REVELATION
James L. Blevins

KNOX PREACHING GUIDES
John H. Hayes, Editor

FROM THE LIBRARY OF
THE INSTITUTE FOR
WORSHIP STUDIES
FLORIDA CAMPUS

John Knox Press
Atlanta

Unless otherwise indicated Scripture quotations are from the Revised Standard Version of the Holy Bible, copyright, 1946, 1952, and © 1971, 1973 by the Division of Christian Education, National Council of the Churches of Christ in the U.S.A. and used by permission.

Library of Congress Cataloging in Publication Data

Blevins, James L.
  Revelation.

  (Knox preaching guides)
  Bibliography: p.
  1. Bible. N.T. Revelation—Commentaries. I. Title.
II. Series.
BS2825.3.B45 1984   228'.07   84-4387
ISBN 0-8042-3250-4

© copyright John Knox Press 1984
10 9 8 7 6 5 4 3 2 1
Printed in the United States of America
John Knox Press
Atlanta, Georgia 30365

Contents

Introduction 1
   Apocalyptic Literature............................ 4
   Theological Geography 6
   Drama in Revelation 7
   Time in Revelation 7
   The Prologue (1:1–8) 8

Visions of the Churches (1:9—3:22) 10
   The Church at Ephesus (2:1–7) 11
   The Church at Smyrna (2:8–11)..................... 14
   The Church at Pergamum (2:12–17)................... 16
   The Church at Thyatira (2:18–29) 19
   The Church at Sardis (3:1–6) 21
   The Church at Philadelphia (3:7–13) 23
   The Church at Laodicea (3:14–22) 25

Visions of the Seals (4:1—8:4) 28
   Vision of Conquering (6:1–2) 32
   Vision of War (6:3–4)............................. 33
   Vision of Famine (6:5–6) 34
   Vision of Death (6:7–8) 35
   Vision of Martyrs (6:9–11) 36
   Vision of Judgment (6:12–17)....................... 37
   Vision of the 144,000 (7:1–17) 38
   Vision of Prayer (8:1–4) 40

Visions of the Trumpets (8:5—11:18) 42
   Destruction of the Greenery (8:7)..................... 43
   Destruction of the Sea (8:8–9) 44
   Destruction of the Rivers (8:10–11) 44
   Destruction of the Heavenly Bodies (8:12) 45
   Destruction Brought by the Eagle (8:13) 47
   Destruction of the Locusts (9:1–12) 47
   Destruction of the Horsemen (9:13–21) 49
   Destruction Foretold in a Scroll (10:1–11) 50
   Destruction of the Outer Temple Courts (11:1–2) 51
   Destruction and Resuscitation of the Witnesses (11:3–14) .. 53
   Destruction of the Destroyers (11:15–18) 54

Visions of Conflict (11:19—15:4) 57
   Satan Versus the Woman and Child (12:1–17) 58
   Satan's Ally: The Sea Beast (13:1–10) 61
   Satan's Ally: The Land Beast (13:11–18) 64

Satan Versus the Lamb (14:1–5)	66
Satan's Allies Warned (14:6–13)	68
Satan Versus the Son of Man (14:14–16)	70
Satan's Allies Judged (14:17–20)	71
Satan's Defeat Celebrated (15:1–4)	72
Visions of Wrath (15:5—16:21)	**74**
Plague on Mankind (16:2)	75
Plague on the Sea (16:3)	76
Plague on the Rivers (16:4–7)	77
Plague on the Sun (16:8–9)	78
Plague on the Beast's Throne (16:10–11)	79
Plague on the Euphrates (16:12–16)	81
Plague on the Air (16:17–21)	82
Visions of Babylon's Fall (17:1—20:3)	**84**
Babylon as a Harlot (17:1–18)	85
Babylon's Doom Foretold (18:1–24)	88
Babylon's Fall Celebrated in Heaven (19:1–10)	92
Babylon's Conqueror (19:11–16)	94
Babylon's Demise Announced (19:17–18)	95
Babylon's Final Battle (19:19–21)	96
Babylon's Leader Enchained (20:1–3)	99
Visions of Fulfillment (20:4—22:5)	**101**
Fulfillment of the Millennium (20:4–10)	102
Fulfillment of Judgment (20:11–15)	107
Fulfillment of Heaven and Earth (21:1–3)	108
Fulfillment of Believers (21:4–8)	110
Fulfillment of the New Jerusalem (21:9–21)	112
Fulfillment of Divine Light (21:22–27)	113
Fulfillment of Divine Life (22:1–5)	114
Epilogue (22:6–21)	**117**
The Authenticity of the Prophet	117
The Imminence of the End	118
The Words of Warning	119
Bibliography	**121**

REVELATION

Introduction

For many people, Revelation has become the lost book of the NT, for its message cannot be comprehended nor its symbolical language understood. Pastors often avoid preaching from the book because of the multitude of interpretations which abound among Christians. No other book of the Bible has been so abused in the teaching and preaching of the local church. Thus many pastors find it easier to avoid Revelation rather than deal with untangling the complex problems presented by the book. Yet, the laypersons in our congregations need help in interpreting Revelation so that they might be freed from the merchants of "gloom and doom" who abuse the last book of the Bible. There are very few good works on Revelation available for laypersons. The choice is between volumes that present Revelation as depicting the future in explicit detail or more scholarly tomes whose language they find difficult to understand.

While many Christian preachers have been silent on Revelation, the secular world has recently discovered the book. Hollywood has produced numerous motion pictures dealing with themes from Revelation. Countless novels also develop themes from the Apocalypse such as the anti-Christ figure, 666, or the battle of Armageddon. People confronted with this bombardment of themes from Revelation often turn to the church for some word of insight. Frequently, however, they encounter a strange and embarrassed silence concerning the Apocalypse. Pastors fear that they might be identified with those who work out Revelation on charts and graphs and have almost every moment of the day catalogued until the end of the world.

There is great need for "sound and sane" preaching from Revelation. The book has a positive message of hope for people facing despair and persecution. Revelation has a timeless message which transcends the first century and the struggles of the Christians within the Roman empire. A victorious spirit is spread throughout the Apocalypse which gives the modern reader the impression that God is in control of world history. On the last page of Revelation stand God and the Lamb—not Caesar, Satan, or any other force. It is interesting that whenever Christians have been persecuted, there has been a renewed interest in reading Revelation. The people in your flock need to be freed from the "doom and gloom" of Revelation and be presented with its positive message.

To avoid the pitfall of those who see only the future tense in Revelation or view it as a predictor of current events, the preacher should devote an introductory sermon to the historical setting of the Apocalypse. First of all, the congregation must understand that Revelation was written for Christians in a setting of political persecution in the first century world, ca. A.D. 95. This information can be presented in an interesting way by means of a role playing sermon of the writer of Revelation—John. Much emphasis should be placed upon the Roman persecution of Caesar Domitian, A.D. 81–96. Domitian believed that he was divine and had statues of himself erected all over the Roman empire. Parts of such a statue have been found at Ephesus. Caesar-worship by citizens throughout the empire provided the means of holding the far flung Roman empire together and gave expression to a common bond of loyalty to the ruler. Although there is not a lot of information available on these persecutions, many scholars believe that Christians were often forced to curse the name of Christ and declare that "Caesar is Lord." Some type of tatoo or marking may have been placed on the worshiper's hand to indicate that he had participated in Caesar-worship. In Revelation thirteen, John seems to indicate such a marking which allows the people to buy food in the marketplace.

Introduction 3

In III Maccabees 2:29, a similar practice emerges when Ptolemy Philopator I (219 B.C.) commanded the Jews to be branded with the sign of Dionysiac worship. From a church father (Tertullian) we learn that a certain Antipas was boiled alive in hot oil in Pergamum because of his refusal to worship Caesar's statue. John as the leader of the churches of Asia Minor was sent into exile on the Isle of Patmos, a Roman political prison in the Aegean Sea. The church father Victorinus declared that John was "condemned to the mines in Patmos by Domitian Caesar where he saw his Apocalypse" (*In Apoc.* 10:11). We even have record of Domitian banishing his own wife Flavia Domitilla to the Isle of Pontus because of her Christian beliefs. Such banishment was a very rigid penalty, for it included chains, scanty clothing, very little food, being kept in caves, and hard labor such as work in rock quarries.

It is evident that the first century persecution by the Roman emperors, especially Domitian, is reflected in the Book of Revelation. One might say there was an organized attempt to abolish Christianity much as what happened to Judaism in the Maccabean period. Above all, Revelation was written from prison to people who were facing prison or execution because of their belief in Christ. The book's message of hope must be heard over against that background.

In doing the role play sermon of John, the preacher can choose one of several identifications for the author of Revelation. Scholars can by no means be certain concerning the identification of John. The traditional view of John the disciple has many points in its favor. From the church fathers, we know that John was the only disciple to die a natural death, at an age of about one hundred years. Eusebius reported that Domitian's persecutions started in the fourteenth year of his reign and "under him the apostle John is banished to Patmos and sees his Apocalypse, as Irenaeus says" (Euscbius' *Chronicle*). In contrast, Dionysius, third century A.D. bishop of Alexandria (Eusebius, *History of the Church*, VII. 25), took pains to point out that there were two church leaders in Ephesus by the name of John. Dionysius made much of the differences in the style and vocabulary between the Fourth Gospel and Revelation leading to the conclusion that the Apocalypse was written by an Elder John not the disciple John. Perhaps the modern scholar Kümmel has expressed the problem the best, "We know nothing more about the author of the Apocalypse than that he was a Jewish-Christian prophet by the name of John" (*Introduction to the New Testament*, p. 331). However, the most important thing is the message of the book not its author.

Apocalyptic Literature

In addition to authorship and dates, the interpreter of Revelation must deal with the fact that the Apocalypse is different in kind from any other in the NT. In our role play sermon of John, we endeavor to bring the hearers into confrontation with the historical setting of Revelation in A.D. 95. Next, it is necessary to deal with the word Apocalypse or apocalyptic. These are words that modern people hear in the secular press but seldom know their exact meaning. The proclaimer must take seriously the fact that the very first word in the Greek text of Revelation is the word *apokalupsis* from which we get our English word Apocalypse or Revelation. To the first-century Christian reader, this word would have brought to mind a whole group of books or a genre of literature that the Jewish people had developed in the last few centuries before the birth of Christ. The word *apokalupsis* means to uncover, reveal, or disclose. Thus, we get our English title for the book—Revelation.

This genre of literature seems to have its origin in the Persian religion and was adopted by the Jews during the exilic and post-exilic periods. From Judaism the literature was taken over by the Christians and became very popular in the early church. In the post-exilic period, the Jewish people were asking why the promises of a golden age for the nation given by the prophets had not materialized. The one answer is found in apocalyptic thought—the golden age will come in a new period of time. Thus, the concept of two ages was very popular in apocalyptic literature. The present age is under the control of evil power and there is little that can be done to redeem it. During this age, the righteous will be persecuted and even condemned to death. Affliction and difficulties will increase up unto the end of the age. However, at some point God will intervene to save his people and inaugurate the new golden age. Apocalyptic literature gives vivid details of this new age and paints glorious visions of a heavenly city or something similar. Those who have become strongly involved in apocalyptic thus take a very pessimistic view of the present world and set their sights on the new world to come.

Along with the two ages, apocalyptic developed a strong dualism—a good God over against an evil one. For example, in Revelation Satan stands over against Yahweh. Satan seems to be the ruler of this age, for he is symbolized with seven heads—divinity and ten horns—complete power (Rev 12). However, Revelation, unlike some Apocalypses, never makes Satan an equal power with God. Even in the final struggle at Armageddon (chap. 19), Satan is never in direct conflict with Christ. An angel actually binds him and places him into the bottomless pit. Yet features of dualism are clearly present in Revelation and play a significant role. In chapters twelve through fourteen, the struggle between Satan and his two monster beasts and the Lamb is very vividly described as a warfare between hostile forces.

Another aspect of apocalyptic literature is its heavy dependence upon visions. In this literature, such experiences usually come to very important people like Abraham, Elijah, or Enoch. These names are actually pseudonyms, donned by the author to bring authority to his visionary experiences. The apocalyptic visions are usually filled with various angelic beings and demonic forces.

In Revelation, there are angels in charge of the water, the winds, and the altar. Demonic forces are in control of the bottomless pit ruled over by the evil angel Abaddon or Apollyon. John's visions of heaven and God's throne room (chaps. 4 and 5) are literally filled with thousands of angelic beings. These visions give to apocalyptic literature a dramatic quality which makes the action alive and real. In Revelation, one of John's most dramatic visions is in chapter twelve—the woman, the child, and the red dragon. There great use is made of color, symbols, and action to make the message very alive and always to be remembered.

In many of the Christian apocalyptic books, there is a Messiah figure as well as an anti-Christ one. In some of the Jewish Apocalypses, the role of Messiah, however, is missing entirely. Sometimes, the position of Messiah becomes subordinate to that of Son of Man such as in Enoch and Revelation. The messianic idea is also expressed in terms of a messianic interim age between the present time and the age to come. In Revelation this is expressed in terms of a thousand-year reign of the Messiah before the introduction of the new Jerusalem. In the Apocalypse of Elijah one finds an interim reign of forty years.

In its final form, apocalyptic literature makes great use of symbols, numbers, colors, animals, and even theological geography. These symbols are almost like codes which need deciphering—at best a special language which needs interpreting. Much of the difficulty in the interpretation of Revelation has to do with its symbolic language being taken literally. Thus it is very necessary to pay attention to these symbols.

Theological Geography

Places and locations in apocalyptic literature have theological meanings and significance. In Revelation the following are significant:

The Sea— symbolizes evil or hostile forces. The beast comes up from the sea, but in the new Jerusalem there is no more sea (Rev 13:1; 21:1).

The Abyss— the home of evil spirits, fallen angels and point of origin for plagues and monster beasts (Rev 9:1).

The Mountain— the site of visions and revelations (Rev 21:10).

New Jerusalem— the center of hope and promises for God's people (Rev 21:10).

The Temple— the dwelling place of God and center of action for many of the visions in Revelation (Rev 11:1).

Lake of Fire— sometimes called the second death and the final dwelling place for evil. Gehenna or hell is never used in Revelation (Rev 20:15).

The Throne of God—a site of holiness and expresses the presence of God. Appears in seventeen chapters of Revelation (Rev 4:2).

Babylon—a code name for Rome or the enemy (Rev 18:2).

Drama in Revelation

Many scholars over the years have recognized a dramatic quality in the Book of Revelation which makes it stand out from other NT books. This dramatic element stems from the fact that Revelation is dealing with visionary experiences. John saw the visions; he heard the beautiful music recorded in the book; he felt the force and power of the presence of God. John could not write down a visionary experience in prose, for he needed a dramatic medium to capture his experiences. He wanted the Christians to relive his experiences as his book was read aloud in the seven churches. The very first blessing (one of seven) in Revelation is directed to the one who reads aloud the words of the book (1:3). The preacher of Revelation must endeavor to recapture as much of this dramatic flair as possible. One of the best ways is to encourage the congregation to read Revelation aloud at one sitting in their homes. Before you preach the first sermon from the book, let them hear for themselves some of the sheer dramatic overtones of Revelation. The French scholar Ellul has expressed well Revelation's dramatic overtones:

> The apocalyptist is first of all a seer while the prophet is a hearer. Of course, the prophet also has visions, but what is important, decisive, are the words which are spoken to him. Of course, the apocalyptist also receives words, but he is first of all the one who sees the personages, the scenes, the scenario of events. (Jacques Ellul, *Apocalypse*, 1977, p. 21.)

Time in Revelation

In Revelation, the cosmic dramatic form provides a timeless setting for the visionary's teaching. The Greek view of history was of a cycle, endlessly repeating itself. Most readers of Revelation have noticed the repetitive cycles of the book. Yet there is also a straight line movement toward a goal taken over from Hebraic thought. By bringing Greek and Hebraic thought patterns together, John has produced a spiral form of action. Cycles repeat themselves but at the same time there is movement toward a goal. It is much like flying in circles while waiting to land at a busy city airport. Even as one circles, the pattern of the movement carries one toward the goal of landing at the airport. Like Greek tragic drama, Revelation has a climactic point near the center of the book and the denouement comes near the end, a structuralist pattern of A B C D C' B' A.' Yet, the movement toward a goal reminds one of prophetic literature.

As a consequence, the time sequence of Revelation should not be relegated to the past as some interpreters have done nor all to the future as many modern interpreters have said. The preacher must go back to the past and discover what the message was in the first century world. From there one must hear a timeless message of truth for every age. At the same time, one must keep in mind that John also foresaw an endtime or conclusion to history.

The timeless dramatic framework of Revelation can be a very helpful one to the preacher in trying to grasp the book as a whole. This approach allows Revelation to stand on its own and be perceived with its own beauty of design. It can be viewed as a work of art painstakingly put together by a brilliant writer, inspired of God. Thus one can avoid the pitfall of making Revelation fit into some scheme taken from Daniel as in some current millennial schools. It is unlikely that John himself had hopes of dramatizing his story on the stage, but he did use the dramatic medium as a means of bringing his message alive to his readers. When the pastor at Ephesus first read Revelation aloud, his congregation could feel through the dramatic medium that they had participated in John's vision and shared in hearing the angelic choir. Before preaching your first sermon from Revelation, read the book aloud at one sitting. Close your eyes from time to time and visualize the action with a cosmic stage in the background. Then preach through Revelation and make it come alive for your congregation.

The Prologue (1:1–8)

Before launching into his great drama, John sets forth a brief introduction to his work. Although short in scope, the section is important in helping us to understand the coming visions of the Apocalypse. First of all, John is concerned to affirm the origin of his work—it comes from God himself (1:1). He further asserts that his words are prophetic and should be read aloud in the churches (1:3). In addition, John underscores his belief that the end of the age is very near (1:1, 3, 7). The one who will be returning is the very one who died on the cross for their sins (1:5–6). In this Prologue, we are introduced to the three main characters of the Apocalypse: the angel interpreter (1:1), Jesus Christ (1:5), and John (1:4).

Visions of the Churches
(Revelation 1:9–3:22)

The symbol of this first section of Revelation is the seven branched golden lampstand. Such a lampstand represents each of the churches which receives a message in the book. John features one theme from the Jerusalem temple in each of the seven divisions of his work. If one pinpoints the seven churches on a modern map of Turkey and draws lines between them, in rough form a seven branched lampstand emerges. Churches that are similar are paired with one another on the lampstand.

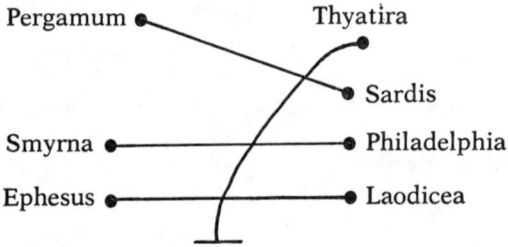

Throughout Revelation, the brilliance of John's writing style is demonstrated by the rich use of symbols like the seven-branched lampstand and the Son of Man figure which he uses as integrating factors. John is in a Roman prison for preaching Christ, so he cannot openly speak about him. Thus in 1:12–20, he uses the Son of Man figure to preach a whole sermon in symbolical color code. The Son of Man figure has hair white as wool or as snow representing his purity. In addition, his garment is adorned with a golden girdle, a color standing for worth or value. His feet are like burnished bronze, symbolizing his great strength. Out of his mouth comes a sharp two-edged sword bespeaking the power of his words. Without openly declaring it, John delivers a vital message about Jesus Christ. In the following seven letters to the churches, John repeats one theme of this Son of Man portrayal in each of the letters in direct relation to the history of the church being featured.

In the early church, this first section of Revelation was often dramatized in the worship service. Such dramatization may well be done by the modern pastor. One needs seven, seven-branched lampstands to represent the seven churches. Have one person dress as the Son of Man in a white robe with a gold band around his/her chest and light the candles in the lampstands. As each candle is set aglow, the pastor reads aloud the appropriate letter to that church. John relates in these letters the strengths and weaknesses of the churches. In Smyrna and Philadelphia, however, there are no weak points and no strong point in Laodicea. However, the lighting of a candle without a word being spoken intensifies this lack of weakness or strength. At the end of the letter, the choir sings: "He who has an ear let him hear what the Spirit says to the churches." At the conclusion of the lighting and reading, the sharing of the bread and cup takes place. This type of observance makes a very beautiful communion service.

A series of seven sermons can be preached on the seven churches of Asia Minor. The following treatment of the churches will provide a basic three point sermon outline for each:

(A) An introductory role play of the mayor of the city in which the basic historical facts and other interesting details are developed about the city. This can be a hook to catch your congregation's interest.

(B) A brief overview of the entire letter to the church follows. One might even read the letter aloud as one candle at a time is lighted on a Menorah.

(C) Finally, one point of the letter is singled out for special comment and application to today's church.

The Church at Ephesus (2:1–7)
"Fallen from First Love"

A role play sermon of the mayor of Ephesus might introduce the first sermon of the series and include the following important facts:

Today, the ruins of ancient Ephesus would lead one to think it was an inland city and had not once been a famous seaport. In biblical days, Ephesus however was a booming seaport town located directly on the Aegean Sea. It lay on a plain stretching east and west, closed in on the north and south by the Gallesion and Koressos mountain ranges. Sailing between the islands of Chios and Samos, one came immediately to the port of Ephesus. Today the entrance to that harbor is closed by a sandy beach brought about by the silt which the Caÿster river deposited in the harbor. The present plain of Ephesus constituted the ancient harbor.

The ruins of Ephesus lie about a mile from the modern Turkish town of Ayasoluk. The records of Ephesus go back to 1100 B.C. when a group of Greek Ionian colonists came and expelled the older population and established a city near the Koressos range. This colony lasted for four centuries, and the colonists began to worship the local deity, Artemis, giving up their adoration of Athena.

A new page in the city's history began in 560 B.C. when Ephesus was conquered by Croesus. This victory represented a change from Greek rule to Anatolian control. During this time a temple to Artemis was designed and built by the architect Chersiphron. In 334 B.C., the city fell to Alexander the Great, and the Greek spirit experienced a revival. During the Anatolian period, the great goddess Artemis was often depicted as a queen bee with her priestesses shown as working bees and her priests as drones. After Alexander, the Greek influence changed the goddess into human form. Artemis was the goddess of wild nature, of the hunter. Her worship included fertility rites involving sexual relations with hundreds of sacred women.

Much of the city as it appeared in John the apostle's day was planned and built by Lysimachus about 294 B.C. He laid out a long street leading from the harbor through the center of town to the base of Mt. Pion. This street was lined by beautiful buildings and porticoes. Near Mt. Pion was located the Great Theater mentioned in Acts 19:29.

In 196 B.C., Ephesus was captured by Antiochus the Great of Syria, and the Asian influence again was felt. The Romans, in turn, took over as they came to power and organized the province of Asia in 133 B.C. Ephesus remained under Roman control except for one brief period in 88 B.C. until it was overrun by the Goths in A.D. 263.

During the Roman period, Ephesus was the chief city of the province of Asia, although Pergamum was the capital. As a seaport it was a gateway to the province and on the main road from Syria to Rome. The Roman governors always entered the province by way of Ephesus. Artemis, the goddess of Ephesus, was also considered to be the deity of the whole province of Asia. Thus, Acts 19:27 states that Artemis is the deity "whom all Asia and the world worship."

Following the role play of the mayor, the sermon continues with a discussion of the message of the letter to the church at Ephesus and a brief word of interpretation about each. (Light one Menorah as you read messages.)

The following is an overview of the letter to Ephesus: The angel of the church is greeted. This angel may be the pastor of the church (2:1a). Just as the Son of Man stands in the midst of the seven lampstands, Ephesus stands in the midst of the seven cities (2:1b). In each of the seven letters some theme of the Son of Man from 1:12-20 is repeated. Great emphasis is placed upon the theme of work and labor. The church is actively at work in the service of the Lord. It has struggled with the false teachers (Nicolaitans) and forced them out of the church. These Nicolaitans were probably a Gnostic group that taught that one could worship Caesar in the flesh and Christ in the Spirit (2:2-3, 6). The church is also criticized by John for leaving its first love (2:4). John always relates brotherly love to love of God. In rooting out the false teachers, the believers have lost in brotherly love (2:4). The call is for the church to repent and do its former work. If not, its official lampstand will be taken away (2:5). The choir chants the music, "He who has an ear, let him hear what the Spirit says to the churches" (2:7a). Those members who overcome or conquer are promised the tree of life in the paradise of God. The Bible begins with a garden and a tree of life and also ends with a similar picture in Revelation. The saints and martyrs will enjoy this paradise along with the lamb (2:7b).

In the third point of the sermon, one aspect of the message to the church at Ephesus should be developed and applied to the modern church. The basic weakness of the Ephesian Church has a very existential message for our own day. The Ephesian Christians were told that they had fallen from their first love. As we have seen, the reason for this falling away had to do with rooting out the false teachers, the Nicolaitans. Love of God is directly related to love of our fellow human beings. True religion cannot just focus upon God but also upon his human creation. Some modern Christians talk of loving God but continue to practice racism or make sexist remarks. The Christian ethical dimension is missing in their lives. Thus love for God must involve putting our brother and sister in first place in our actions and attitudes. It also involves reaffirming the intense commitment which characterized one's first experience with God. The Ephesians had to look back to discover that experience, even though John was calling them to examine the level of their present commitment to God. An examination would show that they were less fervent now than previously. Being in a spiritual rut is a sad situation either at Ephesus in the first century A.D. world or in the present age.

The Church at Smyrna (2:8–11)
"The Long Road"

The initial role play of the mayor of Smyrna might feature the following facts about Smyrna:

Smyrna was founded in about 1000 B.C. as an Aeolian Greek colony. It was soon captured by Ionian Greeks and made into a great city. It was founded on the banks of the Hermus river but fell in 600 B.C. to King Alyattes of Lydia and was destroyed. From 600 B.C. to 290 B.C., Smyrna was a dead city. King Lysimachus, in 290 B.C. refounded Greek Smyrna carrying out a design of Alexander the Great. He placed the city directly by the sea and made it into a maritime and trade center. The city had an inner harbor that could be closed off by a chain and an outer harbor for the mooring of ships.

Smyrna, from early times, counted itself an ally of Rome. It instituted the worship of Rome as early as 195 B.C. when Syria was still a power in the region. The Roman Cicero once said, "Smyrna is the city of our most faithful and most ancient allies." Smyrna also boasted of being "first of Asia in beauty and size." Much of the beauty was due to its orderly arrangement. The streets were laid out in rectangular blocks and were known for the excellence of their paving.

The "crown of Smyrna" was a well-known phrase in the

ancient world. It was a reference to the public buildings on top of Mt. Pagos, the city's Acropolis. Many ancient writers speak of the great beauty of Smyrna. Aristides declared that the city is as a statue sitting with her feet on the sea, and her head rising to heaven and crowned with a circlet of beautiful buildings. A street around Mt. Pagos looked from a distance like a necklace. This was the famous street of gold which ran from the Temple of Zeus to the Temple of Cybele, the mother goddess, patron of Smyrna.

The city was blest with a wonderful climate and location. The western winds, as well as its hilly location 2,500 feet above sea level, kept the city cool in the summer. Smyrna also claimed to be the home of Homer, honoring him by placing his image on their coins and erecting a theater in his honor—the Homereium.

The following is an overview of the letter to Smyrna: A greeting is delivered to the pastor of the church (2:8a). John repeats his words about the Son of Man from 1:18, "... who died and came to life" (2:8b). The city of Smyrna was a dead city between 600 B.C. to 290 B.C. The church is praised for enduring poverty, affliction and the slander of the Jews in the community. John's feeling is so strong against the Jews that he calls them a synagogue of Satan. According to Roman records, a large Jewish community existed in Smyrna and had contributed money for the beautification of the city (2:9). There is no weakness noted about Smyrna. As we have said earlier, the very silence accompanying the lighting of the candles would underline that truth. The church is then warned that Satan will have some of them thrown into prison for ten days—a complete period of time (2:10a). The choir sings, "He who has an ear, let him hear what the Spirit says to the churches" (2:11a). The church is also promised the crown of life if it is faithful unto death. This crown will be a reminder of the city's claim to fame as the crown city of Asia Minor. In addition the church will not be harmed by the second death or lake of fire (2:10, 11b).

The third part of the sermon on Smyrna might stress the church's strength containing a message of perseverance to the end or "he who overcomes." Salvation can be viewed as past, present, and future. One might stress the fact that the reward is offered to the one who endures to the end. Afflictions and difficulties are to be expected along "the long road." Sometimes Christians grow discouraged along the road and give up the quest. Some people have real difficulties in facing rough times and holding their equilibrium. Such difficulties cause them to question God and doubt the nature of their pilgrimage. Doubts can be healthy when they are faced openly and honestly. It must have been very hard for the Smyrnan Christians to resist Caesar-worship or the contempt of their Jewish neighbors. Yet, they persevered, some even endured a period of time in prison.

The church at Smyrna is often considered to be one of the strongest of the seven. Perhaps the major reason for that status was that it had been tested and tried and had not been found wanting. Many modern churches have had the experience that during difficult days of trying to raise money to erect a building, many members sacrificed in time and financial means. As a result, the church flourished and was filled with life. Yet when the new buildings was finished and the excitement waned, the interest as well as attendance diminished in scope. Sacrifice and commitment along the way ensure that the end of the road will be reached. The apostle Paul expressed that thought well, "Forgetting what lies behind and straining forward to what lies ahead" (Phil 3:13).

The Church at Pergamum (2:12–17)
"Living in Satan's Lair"

The introductory part of the sermon might contain a role play of Pergamum's mayor and include the following essential facts:

Pergamum was truly a city built on a hill which dominated the plain of Caicus, and its history went back to the fifth century B.C. Pergamum, however, emerged as a major city in 282 B.C. when Philaterus revolted against King Lysimachus and founded the kingdom of Pergamum. It fell under Syrian control in 222 B.C. when Antiochus the Great conquered it. In 190 B.C., Pergamum came under the rule of the Romans and in 133 B.C. was made the capital of the new Roman province of Asia.

The first temple of the Imperial cult involving the worship of Rome in Asia was built in Pergamum (29 B.C.). This temple appeared on most all of the coins of the city. This city had four patron deities: Zeus, Athena, Dionysus, and Asclepius. The first two represent the Greek influence and the last two, the Anatolian influence.

Pergamum was situated about fifteen miles inland from the Aegean Sea on the Caicus River. Most of the city was built on a hill which was one thousand feet high. It was well-known for its library—second only to Alexandria (Mark Anthony later sent it to Cleopatra as a gift). Our English word parchment comes from the word Pergamum. It was one of the first cities to be planned. Public buildings were placed at the top of the hill and the residential area for the rich was just below the public building. Then came the market place which separated the rich from the poor residential area at the foot of the mountain. In the valley below the mountain stood the famous medical school in connection with the Asclepius cult.

An overview of the letter to Pergamum: A greeting is given to the pastor of the church at Pergamum (3:12a). The sword in the mouth of the Son of Man is featured. Pergamum was known in the ancient world as the city of the sword. John seeks to show the Son of Man as superior to the power of Pergamum. The sword is described as being two-edged just as the words of Christ pierce to the very soul (2:12b). John then praises the great faithfulness of the church in the face of persecution. Evidently, one church member, Antipas, has already been put to death for his refusal to worship Caesar's statue. According to one church father (Tertullian), Antipas was boiled alive in hot oil. The Christian witness in Pergamum was difficult to give because of the throne to Zeus located on the mountain top in the city. It was rather severe for Christians to live in the very shadow of this altar. John refers to that altar as Satan's throne (2:13).

Several weaknesses can be listed about the Pergamum church. False teachers were allowed to circulate in the church. John compares them to the figure Balaam in the Book of Numbers (24:1–2; 31:16). Before the Israelites crossed over into the promised land, Balaam taught them to commit immorality in the Baal cults and to participate in idol worship. John also points to the presence of the Nicolaitans at Pergamum—the same group present at Ephesus (2:14–15). In a warning, the sword motif is reintroduced. If the church does not repent, the Son of man will war against them with the sword coming from his mouth (2:16). The choir then chants the music, "He who has an ear, let him hear what the Spirit says to the churches" (2:17a). The church is also promised the hidden manna and the white stone. Many Jews believed that the manna of Moses' day had been hidden away for the Messianic age. White stones were often used at Pergamum in city elections and for entrance tickets to various events. Thus John is stressing the reward of the possession and entrance into the Messianic age (2:17b).

The final part of the sermon might deal especially with Pergamum's major weakness. False teachers were an obvious threat to that church's existence. Mankind has only a thin veneer of civilization. One might also say the same concerning the true worship of God. Paganism is always "just around the corner." False teachers still are around the church to summon it to reflect a materialistic culture and to bow down to the idols of our own day. American culture can itself become the focus of worship. The Pergamum church was really seeking to find the "easy way out." It was much easier to give in to the prevailing patterns of culture than to stand and give testimony to "him who has the sharp two-edged sword." Satan's throne not only stood in the midst of Pergamum but stands in every community in our present world. There are always modern day Balaams who would call us to give in to the evil of the world around us and accommodate ourselves to the current popular values. There are always voices in every culture which say, "It can't be wrong if everyone else is doing it." In Nazi Germany, it took a lot of courage for some Christians to resist the prevailing anti-Semitic propaganda and even risk their own lives to save Jewish friends and neighbors.

The only problem with Christians giving in or accommodating themselves to prevailing public views is that soon the church loses the ability to speak a prophetic word to its age. Often things like racism can be given a Christian veneer and even Bible verses found to support it. The Nicolaitans at Pergamum were saying, "Give in and worship Caesar so that you may eat." However, Christians over the ages have found that "eating" or being at ease are not the only important things in the world.

Revelation 1:9–3:22 19

The Church at Thyatira (2:18–29)
"Faith at Work"

In the first part of the Thyatira sermon, the dramatic monologue of the mayor might include the following basic facts about the city: Thyatira lay on the road between Pergamum and Sardis to the south and was built on the banks of the Lycus River. This city was located on the most important road in the whole country—the one great route from Pergamum to the east. Thyatira had no natural protection; it served as a protection for the capital city of Pergamum.

It was founded by Seleucus I in 282 B.C. The city worshiped the god, Tyrimnos, who was similar to the Greek god Apollo. He appears on coins on horseback armed with a battle-ax and a club. Thyatira was a great commercial center. More trade-guilds were known here than in any other Asian city. Various inscriptions include the following: wool-workers, linen-workers, makers of outer garments, dyers, leather workers, tanners, potters, bakers, slave dealers and bronze smiths. Lydia, mentioned in Acts 16:14, was from this city and was involved in selling purple cloth.

Thyatira experienced a history of constant destruction and rebuilding. Its unique position as a guard-city for the capital city ensured its life, for even the conqueror felt constrained to rebuild it to guard the newly acquired capital of Pergamum.

An overview of the letter to Thyatira: First, a greeting is given to the pastor of the Thyatira church (2:18a). In this letter, John features the blazing eyes of the Son of man and his bronze feet. These features would remind the readers of the blazing fires of the ovens in Thyatira making bronze and brass. The description would call attention to the great strength of the Son of Man (2:18b). John praises the church for its love and works. In fact their last works are even stronger than their first. The great patience of the church is also underlined (2:19). The church is then criticized for allowing a false prophetess by the name of Jezebel to work in the congregation. This woman may have been a part of the Balaam cult or Nicolaitan group mentioned earlier. The same basic false teaching seems to be present: what one does in the body—eating meat offered to idols or worshiping Caesar's statue—does not harm one's spiritual relationship to Christ (2:20). John gives a strong warning to Jezebel and her followers. If they do not repent, they will be destroyed. In that way all will recognize the mighty power of God (2:21–23). Several rewards or promises are made to the Thyatira church. Those who have avoided Jezebel's false teaching will not receive any other burden. The "deep secrets of Satan" referred to in 2:24 probably are gnostic teaching in which secrets are shared after a period of deep study in these cults. Those who persevere will also receive authority over the nations and the morning star. These rewards signify that one will share in the messianic rule (2:24–27). The choir then chants the music: He who has an ear, let him hear what the Spirit says to the churches" (2:29).

The final segment of the sermon might treat the theme of the mature Christian and be based on the major strength of the church at Thyatira. John mentions that the last works of the Thyatira church are greater than their first. Christian life should be viewed in terms of developing a life style worthy of the faith. In his letters, Paul often spoke of "putting off" certain things and "putting on" other things. Some Christians as they make their pilgrimage do fewer good works rather than more. Somehow, since the time of the Reformation the term "works" has received a bad press. We have heard much about faith and its being the sole element needed for a salvation experience. Yet in the seven letters of Revelation the most popular words are endurance, patience, toil, tribulation, and works. One soon realizes after reading these letters that the faith experience in Christ did not negate the need for a life of righteous works. John commends the Thyatira church because they are accomplishing more works than when they first started their pilgrimage.

The mature Christian realizes the need to express his/her faith in concrete spiritual works. Thus it is good that we have both Paul's letters and the Epistle of James in our NT. Yet it is hard to convince modern Christians of the need to do more good works today than yesterday. James' definition of true religion is still very appropriate, "Religion that is pure and undefiled before God and the Father is this: to visit orphans and widows in their affliction, and to keep oneself unstained from the world" (James 1:27).

The Church at Sardis (3:1–6)
"The Moral Minority"

The opening dramatic monologue of the Sardis mayor might include the following basic facts about the city: Sardis was one of the outstanding cities of ancient history. It was located on a plateau, 1500 feet above sea level which made it an ideal situation to defend. It was like a watch tower overlooking the Hermus plain. Its history goes back to about 1200 B.C. with the beginning of the Lydian kingdom. The city quickly outgrew its mountain-top location and a lower city was built at the foot of the mountain. The old city served as an acropolis. Thus, the city was called by Sardeis, a plural noun. As capital of ancient Lydia, Sardis was very wealthy and thus it had to fight frequent battles. The Greek cities along the coast viewed Sardis as *the* enemy. Its very name stood for power, wealth, and great force.

Hence, the fall of Sardis was earthshaking news in the ancient world. Croesus, king of Sardis, had consulted all the Greek gods and the Delphic Oracle before he went to war with Cyrus of Persia. He crossed the Halys into Persia and was crushed by Cyrus. He retreated back to Sardis to build up an army for the next year. Cyrus surprised everyone by following the Lydians to Sardis and laying seige to the city. King Croesus thought that he now had Cyrus where he wanted him. He retired one night thinking all was well and awakened the next morning to find Cyrus in control of the Acropolis.

The rock which underlay the upper city was limestone—thus very porous—cracking very easily and quickly eroding. Cyrus found such an eroded hole and led his soldiers under the city wall into the heart of the city. Through lack of proper care, this weakness had gone unnoticed by the officials of Sardis. However, the wise Persians were looking for such a place. The people of Sardis were so confident of the impossibility of attack on the steep mountain side of the city that they did not even post a guard there.

History was repeated and the same thing happened again in 230 B.C. when Antiochus the Great of Syria captured Sardis by coming up the unguarded mountain side of the city. Again all the soldiers were posted on the southern wall of the city—the easiest approach to Sardis.

The patron goddess of the city was Cybele—a fertility cult that involved the worship of nature. Two columns of Cybele's temple still stand in Sardis near the Pactolus river. Cybele was thought to have the power of restoring life to the dead. Sardis experienced a harsh earthquake in A.D. 17. It recovered with generous help from the Roman Emperor, Tiberius. During the Roman period, the upper city ceased to be the true city—it was too inconvenient.

The overview of the letter to Sardis: A greeting is delivered to the pastor of Sardis (3:1a). John repeats here the description of the Son of Man holding the seven stars and standing in the midst of the seven lampstands. Ancient Sardis stood on a plateau 1500 feet above sea level. The upper city was built on Mt. Tmolus. On a clear day, the city could be seen for miles across the plain. However, in a similar sense, the Son of Man with the seven stars in his hand stands over the churches (3:1b). A few persons in Sardis have kept their clothing unsoiled. John finds it very difficult to single out anything in the church for praise (3:4a). The works of the Sardis Christians are pointed out for criticism. Their deeds are passive rather than active and have not reached their completion. In fact John refers to them as dead works. Perhaps these Christians started out with enthusiasm but soon fizzled out (3:1c & 2b). The church is warned to become faithful and preserve those things which have not yet died. If not, the Son of Man threatens to come upon them like a thief in the night. Cyrus and Antiochus had come upon the city by stealth, slipping through holes in the rocks under the city wall to take it (3:2a and 3:3). Those who persevere to the end will receive white clothing to wear—a symbol of their immortal bodies. Their names shall not be removed from the Book of Life. The idea of a Book of Life seems to have come from ancient Persia, where such a book contained the names of tax paying citizens. Here in Revelation, it is a list of the true believers who persevere to the end. The promise is also made that these names will also be confessed before God's throne (3:5). The choir then chants the music: "He who has an ear, let him hear what the Spirit says to the churches" (3:6).

One might zero in on the point of strength for the final section of the sermon. The idea of the remnant is a very strong theme in the OT. Here in Sardis, only a few have not been soiled by the city's evil influence. These few have given the true witness and kept the church together. How often do we experience that truth in many modern churches. A few dedicated people labor and persevere so that the work of the church might go on. Some pastors like to play the numbers game and brag of the large numbers in their religious meetings. Yet it remains true that God often has to work through the few or the remnant. The only trouble with a democratic form of government is the fact that the majority is not always right. Sometimes the minority has the correct view and has to persevere to be heard or to amend some wrong action which has been taken.

In ancient Israel, God worked through a remnant who were faithful to his promises and obeyed the covenant. In Sardis, he relied upon a few dedicated Christians to carry out the work. In the history of God dealing with his people, the moral have very seldom been the majority. A few righteous people in every age have been the leaven to change society and influence world powers. Martin Luther King, Jr. in the first days of his struggle to bring equality to the blacks of America seemed at times to be a lone voice in a great desert of unconcern. Yet that lone voice sparked a civil rights revolution in our country. Gains were made that few would ever have thought possible. One should never underestimate the voice of the remnant or the few. Even as at Sardis, they leave their footprints in the sands of concern for that which is right, and they shall be clothed in white.

The Church at Philadelphia (3:7–13)
"The Church of the Open Door"

The introductory dramatic monologue of the Philadelphia mayor might include the following major facts about the city:

This city was named after Attalus II, 159–138 B.C., who was called "Philadelphus" because of his love for his brother Eumenes. It was located in the valley of the Cogamis River, a tributary of the Hermus. The city was founded as a community on the frontier of the Pergamenian kingdom to consolidate, regulate, and educate the barbarians. In particular, it was given the mission to import Greek culture and became very successful in doing that. By A.D. 19, Greek was being spoken in the area and the Lydian language was in disuse.

The main road from Smyrna ran up the Cogamis river past Philadelphia on to the east. The city was built on a broad hill running from the river up to Mt. Tmolus. This city along with Sardis was destroyed in the earthquake of A.D. 17. However, in Philadelphia, tremors continued long after, and for that reason many of the citizens lived outside the city walls in tents and huts refusing to re-enter the city.

An overview of the letter to Philadelphia: A greeting is delivered to the pastor at Philadelphia (3:7). John stresses the keys which the Son of Man holds, described in 1:18.

Philadelphia is seen as having an open door to bring Greek culture to the barbarians. However, the church has before it an even greater door of missionary opportunity, and the Son of Man holds the keys to that door (3:7). The Philadelphia church is perhaps the strongest of the seven. The Christians there have taken advantage of the open door before them. They have not denied the name of Christ. Some of their efforts have been forceful (a little power; 3:8). There is no major weakness in the congregation. If any, perhaps the reference to little power in 3:8 would point to the need for more dedication. The congregation is warned of the imminent return of the Son of Man. That fact is reason enough for a call to perseverance of the Christians (3:11). John says that those of the synagogue of Satan (the Jews) will come and bow down before the feet of the Christians. The faithful will also be kept from the hour of persecution coming upon the earth. They are also promised that they will be pillars in the temple of God. What a secure reward for frightened people living in tents outside the city wall. God's name will be written on his own people (3:9–10, 12). The choir chants the music: "He who has an ear, let him hear what the Spirit says to the churches" (3:13).

The final part of the sermon might be built around this city's vision of the Son of Man and the emphasis on the open door motif within the letter. Thus, there is within the letter a strong concern for missions. The city was built by non-Christians to bring Greek culture to the barbarians. The Christian church there had the mission to bring the message of God's love to these same people. Only in Christ could the city really live up to its name. The name of the city itself, Philadelphia means "brotherly love." The mission of the church must always be one of love and concern for the whole world. The church has survived all of these hundreds of years because it sought to reach out and break down barriers along the way. Frank Stagg (*The Book of Acts*, 1955) has shown that the early church broke down three major barriers as the church reached out from Jerusalem and pushed on to Rome, the capital city of the empire. The first barrier fell to the Samaritans, the second to God-fearing Gentiles, and the third to pagan Gentiles at Antioch. When the last barrier fell, it was like a dam bursting—the Gospel spread around the shore of the Mediterranean Sea finally reaching Rome itself.

The little church at Philadelphia like its sister congregation at Antioch dared to dream the impossible of confronting the whole Roman world with the Gospel. Barriers of race, sex, and economic status still exist in many of our modern churches. The Gospel yet possesses the power to break down these barriers and allow the Christian message to be truly an open door to all who would come and enter through it. The message of Christ has always been a universal one.

The Church at Laodicea (3:14–22)
"Neither Hot nor Cold"

The role-play in the first part of the sermon might feature the mayor of Laodicea and contain the following facts about the city:

Laodicea was founded by Antiochus II, 261–246 B.C. and named in honor of his wife—Laodice. It was built to guard the great road to the east from Ephesus which ran through its center. It was located in the Lycus valley directly across the river from Hierapolis and twelve miles down stream from another biblical city, Colossae. However, its greatest weakness was that it lacked an adequate supply of water in time of seige.

Laodicea was well-known in the Roman world as a banking and manufacturing town. The Lycus Valley was noted for its wool—soft and glossy black in color and from thus a popular line of clothing was manufactured in the empire. In Laodicea stood a famous temple to the Phrygian god—Men Karou which contained a school of medicine. The school was known all over the Roman empire for its ear medicine and eye salve. The Laodicean physicians in the school followed the teaching of Herophilos (330–250 B.C.). There was also a large Jewish population here in Roman times. In 62 B.C., the Roman governor of Asia refused to allow the Jews at Laodicea to send a collection to Jerusalem. The money taken from them would point to an adult Jewish population of 7,500.

The overview of the letter to Laodicea: The message is directed to the pastor of the church (3:14a). John repeats the description from the Son of Man in 1:5. The city of Laodicea was the wealthiest of the seven and also seemed to contain the weakest church. Thus, the Christians need to be reminded that the Son of Man is the true and faithful witness. He is the beginning of creation—not Laodicea (3:14b). As this candle is lighted, there is silence. John can think of nothing to praise at Laodicea. Of course, there is much to criticize. The church's works are just like their city's water supply—lukewarm. To overcome its lack of water, the city built aqueducts to hot springs (95 degrees) two miles or more from the city. These springs may have contained sulphur. By the time this 95 degree water reached the city it was lukewarm. The church also brags about being rich but John points out that in reality, it is "wretched, pitiable, poor, blind, and naked" (3:17). The church is warned that if they remain as they are (lukewarm), the Son of Man will vomit them out of his mouth. John warns them to buy refined gold, put on white clothing, and use salve on their eyes. These directions stand in direct parallel with the city's claim to fame—it's banks, clothing industry and famous eye salve. There is one final warning that because God loves them he will reprove and chasten them (3:16, 18–19). The Lord will come in and dine with them if they are willing to open the door. The Christians of Laodicea will also sit with Christ on his throne if they persevere to the end (3:20–21). The choir then chants the music: "He who has an ear, let him hear what the Spirit says to the churches" (3:22).

The third point of the sermon should emphasize the warning given to the church. The theme of "lukewarm" is one we encounter in all areas of life. Intensity and commitment often seem to be lacking in our human experiences. The term "lukewarm" is even more distressing when it is applied to Christians. The faith has gone forward because of the willingness of Christians even to risk their lives for the faith. The wealth of Laodicea provides many points of contact with our own contemporary American culture. The NT contains many strong passages directed at the rich.

Of course, money itself is not evil but rather the use which is made of it. It is obvious that at Laodicea, the wealth of the congregation has dulled the sharp edge of commitment found in some of the other churches of Asia Minor. The zeal of Smyrna or Philadelphia is missing in Laodicea.

Someone has asked the question in relation to wealth, "When is enough, enough?" Does true Christian commitment reflect itself in a simpler life style? Would one's Christian testimony shine brighter if one consumned less beef so that the grain used in feeding animals might be used to feed the hungry of third world countries? There is nothing worse than lukewarm commitment to a cause. It is interesting to note that throughout its history the Christian Gospel has waxed strong in periods of persecution. In Revelation, Laodicea seemed to be a church that faced no persecution nor hardship, for on the contrary it shared in the wealth of the city. At the same time, however, it receives some of the harshest criticism of the seven churches. Many of our American churches are known for their great wealth but are also known for their lack of concern for the needy of the world. The worse examples are some of the modern electronic churches that yearly earn millions of dollars in donations but have no ministries to people in need.

The Visions of the Seals
(Revelation 4:1—8:4)

In chapter four John is caught up to heaven and beholds the throne room of God. John takes two whole chapters (4 and 5) to describe this experience in some detail. It is a scene of worship and music and its dominant central feature is the throne of God. One can not really see the form on the throne—a bright jewel like jasper or carnelian casts bright rays blinding the beholder. One cannot see God but only a scroll with seven seals which he has in his hand. Around the throne, John beholds four living creatures, one with the face of a lion, one with the face of an ox, a third with a man's face, and a fourth with an eagle's face. God is surrounded by his creation: the lion representing the wild creatures; the ox, the domesticated creatures; man, intelligent life; and the eagle, the flying creatures. These creatures which remind us so much of the figures in OT prophetic visions have six wings.

In addition to the four living creatures, John views twenty-four elders also sitting on thrones. They serve as the choir in Revelation singing music and interpreting the drama. Several interpretations of these twenty-four elders exist. The most likely seems to be that they represent the old covenant and the new covenant, or the twelve tribes and the twelve apostles. Later in 21:12 and 14, John will see the names of the tribes on the twelve gates of the city and the twelve apostles' names on the foundation stones of the city. Thus, John is preaching a sermon in symbolic language—God surrounded by his creation, and God's covenants (old and new) given to that creation. A trinitarian formula is also present, for Father, Son, and Holy Spirit are represented in this scene. The seven burning torches in front of the throne stand for the Holy Spirit, for throughout the Bible, fire is a symbol for the Spirit of God. We have already viewed God on his throne. The Lamb with seven horns and seven eyes, symbolizes Christ. The seven horns stand for his divine power and the seven eyes for divine sight. Thus the throne room scene contains Father, Son, and Holy Spirit.

God's throne room resounds with music. The four living creatures begin by singing a hymn of praise to the holy God:

> "Holy, holy, holy, is the Lord God Almighty,
> who was and is and is to come!" (4:8)

This first hymn might introduce a sermon entitled "Holy, Holy, Holy." Worship of God must always have its beginning in a declaration of God's holiness. In a world where God's name is so often taken in vain, it is inspiring to hear the four living creatures sing of God's holiness. God is holy because he is the all powerful righteous force of the universe. So many of the gods which humans worship are weak and unable to influence the destinies of people. We create objects with our hands and then fall down to worship them. Another reason for the holiness of God is the fact that his righteousness is eternal—"who was and is and is to come!" The God of Abraham, Isaac, and Jacob is also our God. Our creator has revealed himself in history and can thus be called a God of history. As Christians we do not worship a ghost, but one who revealed himself in human form in Jesus of Nazareth. In response to God's holiness, individuals must hear the call "to be holy even as He is holy." Any less response is inappropriate to the grand and glorious music of the four living creatures.

The second hymn follows with the twenty-four elders praising God as the creator:

> "Worthy art thou, our Lord and God,
> to receive glory and honor and power,
> for thou didst create all things,
> and by thy will they existed and were created" (4:11).

This second hymn uplifts the creative power of God. In a sermon called "The Creating God" one might delineate the following themes for preaching: (1) God's creative power is a manifestation of his love for his creatures. He brought us into being and gave us the capabilities to see, hear, and perceive. He surrounded us with a cosmos of color, sound, and unbelievable sensations. One can say with the psalmist,

> The earth is the LORD's and the fulness thereof,
> the world and those who dwell therein;
> for he has founded it upon the seas,
> and established it upon the rivers (Ps 24:1-2).

(2) God continues to show his love for us by constantly renewing the world about us. He has not set the world in motion, only to go off and leave it on its own. Each day he renews his world and makes it an even better place in which to live. (3) God's creative power will one day be manifested in a new world in which his creation will be manifest in all of its perfection. Paul was correct in declaring that now we see "through a glass darkly" for our own sin obstructs our vision of God's beautiful paradise in which he has placed us.

At this point in the action, John beholds the scroll with the seven seals in the hand of God. The question is asked, "Who is worthy to open the scroll and break its seals?" (5:2). No one in heaven or earth is found worthy. Then John begins to weep, and one of the elders declares, "Lo, the Lion of the tribe of Judah, the Root of David, has conquered, so that he can open the scroll and its seven seals" (5:5). The Lamb then takes the scroll and as he does the choir sings a third hymn, in honor of the Lamb:

> "Worthy art thou to take the scroll and to open its seals,
> for thou wast slain and by thy blood didst ransom men for God
> from every tribe and tongue and people and nation,
> and hast made them a kingdom and priests to our God,
> and they shall reign on earth" (5:9–10).

"The Lamb as Redeemer" would be a good sermon title that would enable the preacher to focus on some of the key aspects of Christ's ministry. First of all the redemptive mission of Christ is based upon his willingness to surrender his own life for the sins of mankind. Through his death he brings human beings into a proper relationship with God. Christ is worthy to open the scroll in the hand of God because he experienced the same death and pain of the Christian martyrs. Secondly, his redeeming work is for all mankind—"from every tribe, and tongue and people and nation." God's love for his people knows no racial or national barriers. His gift of redemption is for all, everyone who desires it. A modern hymn expresses that thought so well:

> In Christ there is no East or West,
> In Him no South or North;
> But one great fellowship of love
> Throughout the whole wide earth (John Oxenham).

Thirdly, Christ's redeeming work brings about a royal priesthood of believers. Those who respond to Christ's redemptive mission enter a dedicated group of men and women who champion God's love throughout the world. They have direct access to the Father and reign with him.

Then thousands of angels join in the fourth hymn of praise to the Lamb:

> "Worthy is the Lamb who was slain, to receive power and wealth and wisdom and might and honor and glory and blessing!" (5:12).

The music of this hymn inspired Handel to write *The Messiah*. The words might also bring inspiration for a sermon: "Worthy is the Lamb." The Lamb is worthy first of all because he was slain. His death on the cross demonstrated his willingness to follow the will of God and complete his mission. Throughout Revelation John uses the phrase "who was slain" to identify the Lamb to his readers. In chapter seven, John declared that the martyrs "have washed their robes and made them white in the blood of the Lamb" (v. 14). Secondly, the Lamb is worthy to receive the gifts of power, wealth, wisdom and might. These are gifts that any world ruler might desire. Christ uses these gifts to carry out the rule of God. Similar attributes are given to God in the later worship scene in 7:12. Thirdly, the Lamb is worthy to receive the worship of human beings—"honor, glory, and blessing." Because the Lamb has carried out the purposes of God, he is worthy to receive the praises of God's creation. This worship scene almost explodes as thousands of angels swell the heavenly chorus, for the Lamb is the full expression of God in the world.

Finally, everyone in the universe joins in the fifth hymn of praise to God and the Lamb:

> "To him who sits upon the throne and to the Lamb be blessing and honor and glory and might for ever and ever!" (5:13).

The throne of God is an important concept in Revelation and symbolizes the presence of God. A very interesting sermon might be developed around that theme—"To Him who Sits on the Throne." One would first stress the throne of majesty. The reader is somewhat overwhelmed by the description of

God's throne in Revelation. Lightning and thunder come forth from it, and it is guarded by four living creatures with six wings each and eyes all over. The throne is a symbol teaching that God reigns in power and grandeur. The "one who sits on the throne" is definitely the ruler of the universe. Secondly, the throne of mercy should be underlined. The martyrs stand before the throne and receive the gracious care of the Lord—"and he who sits upon the throne will shelter them with his presence" (7:15). The throne of God symbolizes his love and care for his creatures. At God's throne there is no more hunger, pain, or despair. Thirdly, the proclaimer should be aware of the throne of judgment. God's judgment is fearful to some because it brings to light their own evil and moral failure. The unrighteous cry out to the mountains and rocks, "Fall on us and hide us from the face of him who is seated on the throne" (6:16). All these aspects of God's throne are manifest in the fifth hymn of Revelation sung by God's whole universe.

The Lamb then goes forward to take the scroll from the hand of God and to open its seals. The four living creatures say, "Amen." The first four seals and the last three go together, for John likes a basic four-three pattern. The horses symbolize the basic forces in world history: conquering, warfare, famine, and death. Revelation makes use extensively of the cyclical view of history espoused in Greek tragic drama. It is like standing and watching a carousel turn—observing the horses go by. As the wheel of history has turned, mankind has encountered conquering, warfare, famine and death, over and over again. John saw these forces at work in his own day and time. The Romans had marched their armies across the Mediterranean World, and very few countries had escaped the shadow of their power. Roman soldiers were a common place sight in Ephesus, Pergamum, and the other cities of Asia Minor.

Vision of Conquering (6:1–2)

The white horse is a fitting one to symbolize conquering, for the returning victorious Roman general often rode a white horse during the victory parade. In Revelation, the rider of the white horse is given a bow. The Romans, as well as their ancient enemies the Parthians, were very adept at using the bow. It was the major instrument of warfare in the first century world. How many times have we seen this white horse ride across the stage since 1900? Every age has been marked by its conquerors, from Alexander the Great to Hitler. At times, world history seems to be only a long list of names of those who have conquered. One wonders about all the common people who were caught up in the forces generated by these great men of history but who remain without names. Although John saw only the forces of his own time, his description of the white horse has a timeless significance for all of human history.

A sermon title, "The Horse of Conquering" could deal with the theme of the abuse of political power and the resulting affliction brought upon mankind. The history of the world has been punctuated over and over again by great figures desiring to control political kingdoms. One of the temptations which Satan placed before Jesus was that of political power. Jesus might have used his power to control the political kingdoms of the world, but he rejected that temptation. One also sees in the white horse the desire to control human beings. The longing of world conquerors has been to bring the masses under their control. Rome was known in the ancient world for its enslavement of millions of men and women, for the power of the Caesars rested upon a vast human network of slavery. Last of all, the desire for a crown often motivates the conquer. He desires more than political power and control of the masses but also an adulation that borders on worship. It is no wonder that all the Caesars were tempted to call themselves divine. After every military expedition, it was almost mandatory for the Roman general to parade the "fruit of his conquest" through the streets of Rome to elicit the praise and glory of the masses. Over against the white horse of conquering in Revelation stands the white horse bearing Christ. His word is his sword and his crown is one of suffering and pain.

Vision of War (6:3–4)

Following the white horse one would expect to find the red horse of war. Power hungry Caesars often brought the shadow of war into first century communities. Pride and individual greed were forces which pushed conquerors on to the brink of war. Note how many wars our own generation has known since 1900. Jesus once spoke of the endless cycle of wars and rumors of war (Mark 13:7). Much of the horror of World War II was brought upon our globe by Hitler's personal lust for power. The force of war which John viewed in his own day is very real and evident in all ages of world history.

Even now mankind is threatened once again by this reappearing red horse. The world stands on the brink of nuclear disaster. Both Russia and America have enough weapons to destroy the whole world many times over again. Christians throughout the ages have had to live in the midst of the white horse or the red horse. It has been in that kind of world that believers have had to give their witness to the peace of Christ.

This passage concerning the red horse could be used to preach a sermon on the Christian call to peacemaking. Within the cycle of "wars and rumors of wars" one sees the endless cycle of peacemaking. Christians are to be the salt of the earth—ones who speak of peace while others speak of war. It is much easier in our modern age to speak of the need for the arms race than the dire necessity for peace between the nations of the earth. One can either lie back and be trampled by the white or red horse or stand and resist these evil impulses of world history. Jesus stood against even the armed might of Rome and called his disciples to be peacemakers.

Vision of Famine (6:5-6)

The black horse represents famine. The Roman world knew well the meaning of hunger. World history has shown that after every major war there has been famine on the earth. John points to the intensity of the famine by allowing one of the four living creatures to say, "A quart of wheat for a denarius, and three quarts of barley for a denarius; but do not harm oil and wine!" (6:6). A denarius in the first century was worth about twenty cents in our money. Unlike today, however, twenty cents represented a day's wages for a typical working man. A quart of wheat was the daily ration for a Roman soldier of the first century. Yet a working man had to feed his whole family on that amount. Barley was a less expensive grain and perhaps a working man could feed his family with that ration. In many Roman famines, the rich had plenty of olive oil and wine while the poor died of hunger. World famine remains a problem in our modern world. Even in America where there is so much abundance, hunger is still a real dilemma among the poor. The church must always address itself to the issue of hunger and famine in the world. One might preach a sermon on "Faith as a Verb—not just a Noun." Faith as an active verb includes concern for the problem of hunger in the world. The first point might deal with the fact that verbs are more forceful than nouns. We often express our Christian concern in terms of nouns—love, brotherhood, or fellowship. True Christian feeling needs to be declared in to love, to care, or to participate. Verbs insist that action takes place. Secondly, the Christian verb is always active, not passive. Christian concern involves the subject doing the action—being involved in feeding the hungry of the world. For too long, we have considered the black horse to be a necessary part of living in the world. Yet the Christian has the command of Christ to feed the hungry and give drink to the thirsty. James expressed it well in declaring that a Christian must say more to a hungry person than "be ... filled" (2:16). An active verb is needed like "I *will give* you something to eat." Thirdly, an active verb takes an object. It is sometimes easy to give a few dollars to a favorite charity but more difficult to pick out one person in your own community who is hungry. The black horse has left its imprint on human history, but Christians are called to stop its ravages.

Vision of Death (6:7-8)

When the fourth seal is opened a pale green horse appears on the stage. The Greek word *chloros* points to a yellow-green color, the color of a corpse on the battlefield. Hades representing the world of the dead follows behind the horse of death. The underworld (Hades) was a source of fascination for the Greeks and feared by the Hebrews. In the early years of Judaism, the popular expectation was that all would enter into the realm of the dead where one would have at best a shadowy existence. Later the Hebrews developed a belief in life after death. However, even in Jesus' time the Sadducees did not accept the existence of an afterlife.

One might expect the final horse to be this one—the pale

green horse of death. Conquering warfare, famine, and death was a cycle which John had seen many times in his world. In a timeless sense this cycle has been repeated in every age. Many in the present generation have many directly affected in their families by the loss of relatives on the battlefields of World War I, World War II, The Korean War, and the Viet Nam War. World famine has also brought its harvest of death. The New Testament thus places great emphasis upon the conquering of death through Christ Jesus. A sermon on death might well contrast the pale green horse with the victorious Lamb. In the midst of the four horsemen, the Lamb stands firmly and securely. This fact gave great hope to the Christians of the seven churches who were perhaps inclined to think that they would fall under the sway of these mighty forces.

The throne of God is mentioned in almost every chapter of Revelation. Like the Lamb, the throne represents God's presence and concern for his own people in the midst of the forces of upheaval on the face of the earth. Revelation is thus not a book of fear but one of genuine hope. God's love and concern for his people is constant and abiding. This timeless truth needs to be heard in our own generation, for the threat of nuclear war and the forces of upheaval in our own time leave people filled with doubt and uncertainty. Like the Christians of the seven churches of Asia Minor, modern Christians also need to know the love and concern of God for his people. Some constancy is needed in the rapid change of modern history and the fast pace of modern living.

Vision of Martyrs (6:9–11)

In the midst of the forces brought by the four horsemen—conquering, warfare, famine, and death, we now see the Christian martyrs in heaven under the altar of sacrifice. In each part of Revelation, John stresses some theme from the Jerusalem temple, because in the worship ritual of the Jews, the temple played a very important role. Many believed the original model of the temple was in heaven. The main altar of sacrifice stood about fourteen feet tall in the Court of Priests with a ramp leading up to its heights. There the priests would slaughter the sacrificial animals which had been brought to the temple, and the blood of the animals was thrown against the base of the altar. In Revelation, the blood of the martyrs is thrown against the base of the heavenly altar. The martyrs reside under the altar and cry out: "O Sovereign Lord, holy and true, how long before thou wilt judge and avenge our blood on those who dwell upon the earth?" (6:10).

The martyrs play a significant role in Revelation. The Greek word translated as "witness" in English is the term *martus* (martyr). In the early church to give your witness meant to stake your life on what you believed. The martyrs are the ones who do not give in to Caesar Domitian and do not worship his image, and they also rule with Christ in the millennium. Some have criticized their call for revenge against the Romans as being "un-Christlike." Yet, if you had been living in one of the seven cities of Revelation and had experienced persecutions and even the loss of "loved ones" in death, perhaps you would want to join in the martyrs cry of revenge. It seems a natural response to the horror they had experienced.

This section of Revelation lends itself to dealing with martyr theology in the church today. Because of the abuse of that kind of theology in the early church, we seldom hear it mentioned in the modern church. Yet there is a positive message to be heard in terms of staking your life on what you believe. John did not have in mind for the Christians to go out and seek death but rather not to allow death to stand in the way of their Christian witness. Great movements in world history have gone forward because of the willingness of participants to give up their lives for the cause. There have been very few periods of Christian history unmarked by the blood of martyrs. One might preach a sermon on the martyr theme, "Witness Unto Death:" (1) the proclamation of the witness (1:9), (2) the struggle of the witness (7:14), and (3) the victory of the witness (7:9–10).

Vision of Judgment (6:12–17)

God tells the martyrs under the altar that he will not judge the world until their number is complete (6:11). When the last martyr has died then God will judge wicked Rome. This scene is prophetic in nature, for it is a preview of what God's judgment will be like. John uses all the symbols of apocalyptic literature: the sky rolls up like a scroll, the sun turns black as sackcloth of hair, and the moon red as blood. Actual judgment does not take place here, but rather there is a promise given that when God does judge the world, it will be total and complete.

"Cosmic Judgment" is a good title for a sermon dealing with God's ultimate judgment of the world. We see in this passage that God's judgment is universal. No aspect of God's creation escapes the judgment of God: the stars, moon, and the sun are affected by God's righteous power. Even the mountains and islands react in fear and are removed from their places. Secondly, God's judgment falls upon all people dwelling on the face of the earth—"kings of the earth and the great men and the generals and the rich and the strong, and every one, slave and free" (6:15). Those who have taken hold of power and abused it must stand before the great king and be judged on their administration. However, above all, judgment is viewed as a promise given to the martyrs. Those Christians who had suffered so much needed to know that God would avenge their blood. The unrighteous will not always prosper. The Roman empire would not always dominate the world. As cosmic judge, God will determine the course of human history and the world. His word is the last word—"who can stand before it?" (6:17).

Vision of the 144,000 (7:1-17)

Before the judgment of God comes on Rome, it is necessary for all Christians to be sealed on their foreheads. The number 144,000 (12 × 12 × 1000) is a whole number and symbolizes all true believers. John borrows the idea from Exodus where the plagues of Egypt came upon the Egyptians but not the Israelites. Before the tenth plague of death to the first born son, the Israelites placed the blood of the lamb on their doorposts. Here in Revelation, the blood of the lamb is placed on the foreheads of the Christians and protects them from the coming trumpet plagues of the next section of Revelation. It does not protect them from the need to suffer and die for their testimony, but rather from the coming judgment of God.

The theme "The Seal of God" provides many ways of looking at God's love and concern for his people. First one might reflect upon the universality of the seal. It is not intended to mark off some super elect number of saints but rather all who have been redeemed by the Lamb. In Christianity there are no ranks within the church. We are all one in the unity of the cross. The number 144,000 itself symbolizes the totality of the faithful. There is also the witness of the seal. It bespeaks the fact that those who bear the seal have been redeemed. They are on the side of God in the struggle with evil. Satan's forces also bear a mark—the mark of the beast. The mark of the Lamb might well be the cross itself. Those who have been redeemed know the importance of the death of Christ in bringing believers into the presence of God. Finally one might speak of the promise of the seal. Basically, the sealing affords protection from the coming trumpet plagues which are ready to fall upon the world. The seal does not serve to protect the Christians from persecution and hardship. As we see later in chapter seven, the sealed Christians are martyred and march into heaven in a victory parade. The sealing tells us that God will not forget his own and will shepherd them into his kingdom.

John makes use of the new Israel theme in the sealing of the Christians. The early believers viewed themselves as the new Israel of God. The divine promises made to Israel were now being fulfilled in the church. Thus, John lists the tribe of Judah, the Messiah's tribe as first. The total number of 144,000 symbolizes the whole number of Christians. In chapter seven we see the church militant and the church triumphant, for in a broad sweep of history, we view the martyrs facing their persecution on earth and then entering heaven singing triumphal hymns (7:10 and 7:12). Those who pay this high and noble price will be comforted by the Lamb (7:15–17).

In a sermon, "The Church Militant and Triumphant," one might stress some of the important themes concerning the Christian martyrs. In the first point, one could develop the theme of the new Israel. The church is the called out people of God—the chosen or the elect. The early church thus saw an obvious connection between the old Israel and the new Israel. One might point out the reordering of the tribes in Revelation 7 in order to place stress on Judah, the tribe of the Messiah. The second point should emphasize the idea of the church militant—striving and working in the world to establish the righteousness of God. The highlight would of course fall on the martyrs or those who are willing to surrender their own lives for the testimony of Christ. When they die, they have a special place reserved for them under the altar in heaven. In the third point, the concept of the church triumphant should be developed based upon Rev 7:9–17. From the blood and toil of earth, our eyes are turned to heaven as the martyrs march in from their persecution and receive their white robes and rest from their afflictions. Even the death of Christians cannot stop the cause of Christ on earth.

Vision of Prayer (8:1–4)

The seventh seal brings a half hour of silence in heaven. Then seven angels are given seven trumpets. As they prepare to blow them, another angel brings out a golden incense container filled with the prayers of God's people on earth. The angel then fills the empty incense container with hot coals and throws them out on the face of the earth in preparation for the seven trumpet plagues. In the midst of their persecution, the prayers of God's people will be heard. This message brought hope to the Christians in the seven churches who were facing hardship and difficulty because of their witness to Jesus Christ.

"A Half Hour of Silence" would be an interesting sermon title to introduce some thoughts concerning silence before God's revelation. One might first point out that silence is an appropriate reaction to the presence of God. So much of our world revolves around noise. It is impossible to find many places of retreat from the blare of radios and the noise of television commercials. Zechariah expressed it well, "Be silent, all flesh, before the LORD" (Zech 2:13), or as the Psalmist once declared of God, "Be still, and know that I am God" (Ps 46:10). Secondly, one should learn that often God speaks in the silence. We usually remember the experiences of Moses or Isaiah who heard the audible voice of God, but we also have the words of the Psalmist, "commune with your own hearts ... and be silent." (Ps 4:4). God does speak in the silence as well as the spoken word. Thirdly, silence teaches us to anticipate and expect even greater revelations from God. Patience is sometimes a virtue that is very hard to acquire.

Humans by their very nature want to know the future even before it arrives. Americans spend thousands of dollars on fortune telling, horoscopes, and predictions. Even books on Revelation that predict the future outcome of world history—what nations will play what roles—are runaway bestsellers. Yet sometime God is silent and we must wait, but it is not a silence of despair but one of hopeful assurance.

The seven seal visions are not filled with gloom and doom. A sermon might be preached on this whole section 4:1–8:4 stressing the messages of hope. In the midst of conquering, warfare, famine, and death, Christians must give their testimony even unto death. Yet God has promised: (1) his great judgment (6:12–17), (2) his sealing of the martyrs (chapter 7), and (3) his hearing of the persecuted's prayers (8:1–4). God is in control of the history of the world and will bring it to an end according to his own plan. On the last page of human history one will not find Caesar but rather the Lamb!

In this chapter, we have seen the very throne room of God—God surrounded by the heavenly host. It was a scene of majesty and worship as hymn after hymn rung forth from the throne. In the midst of the adulation and worship, we were introduced to Christ. He appeared in the guise of a Lamb with seven horns and seven eyes—a Lamb that had been slain. The Lamb took the scroll in the hand of God and prepared to open it. With the breaking open of the seals, we saw the cause of human history and the forces that would determine it. The first four seals brought the forces of conquering, warfare, famine and death sweeping across the stage. The world has seen those four scourages over and over again. The cyclical nature of history is evident. In the midst of those forces, the focus in seal five fell upon the Christian martyrs. In the midst of the four horsemen, the Christians in every age give their testimony even unto death and join the elect group of martyrs under the altar in heaven. Then the martyrs were given the assurance that God one day would judge the world (seal six) and that they bore the seal of God's protection (Interlude) and that their prayers were heard daily before God's throne (seal seven). Thus, the seal visions bring no message of fear but rather one of hope.

Visions of the Trumpets
(Revelation 8:5—11:18)

The seven trumpets of Revelation bring the first of the plagues upon the earth. In the background fire and smoke, symbolizing judgment, go up from the altar of incense. John foresees that the forces of nature will rebel against the sins of Rome. The blood of the martyrs is on the hands of the Romans; thus in reality, they have brought God's judgment upon themselves. John does not view God as some Roman deity throwing down thunderbolts from Mt. Olympus, rather, nature comes to the support of God's people. One is reminded of similar episodes in the OT where nature aided the Israelites against their enemies (Josh 10:11-13). In fact the ten plagues on Egypt which are similar to the ones in Revelation portray the natural elements warring against the Egyptians.

In Gibbon's book, *The Decline and Fall of the Roman Empire*, three reasons are given for the fall of Rome: (1) natural calamities, (2) inner rot and decay, and (3) invasion of the barbarians. The first four trumpets in Revelation deal with natural calamities. The fifth trumpet symbolizes the inner rot and decay in terms of monster locusts coming out of a pit. The sixth trumpet depicts the invasion of a monster army of two hundred million.

In a cyclical timeless sense, the message of the seven trumpets is relevant for all ages. In one way of looking at things, man's sin is related to his environment. Paul declared in Rom 8:21, "the creation itself will be set free from its bondage to decay and obtain the glorious liberty of the children of God." Paul believed that not only man but the whole universe needed to be redeemed. Man's fall has in some way affected all of mankind. Hence this section of Revelation lends itself to a series of sermons on ecology. Modern man has begun to realize what he has done to the world that God entrusted to him. Just as John saw the world crying out against the sin of Rome, the modern world screams out against the abuse brought about by human beings. In each trumpet plague, one third of things are destroyed. In Revelation fractions represent incompleteness. The purpose of God's incomplete judgment is to give mankind time to repent. All of the trumpet visions undergird God's great mercy, since he restrains his judgment out of love for his people. Yet at the end of the trumpets, people curse his name rather than praise it. We will see that basic message in each of the trumpet plagues.

Destruction of the Greenery (8:7)

Hail, fire, and blood fall upon the greenery of the earth. In John's day, such phenomena were not entirely strange. The red sands blowing from the Sahara desert would at times cause reddish rain to fall around the Mediterranean countries. However, in a spiritual sense, John is saying that the earth's greenery itself reacts in horror to Rome's sin. In the timeless meaning of mankind's sin affecting all of the universe, an ecological sermon might stress what human beings have done to the greenery of the world. Acid rain from the Ohio Valley has caused great damage to the greenery of the northeastern United States and Canada.

This sermon could be entitled, "He Leadeth Me to Green Pastures." The first point should emphasize the "promise of green pastures" from Ps 23. The greenery of our earth symbolizes its very life. The essence of the creation story is found in God's bringing forth a beautiful garden which would be for man's dwelling place. Mankind was given dominion over the garden and its various forms of life but was never to abuse it or misuse it. The second point of the sermon should underline the "abuse of green pastures." In many areas of the world once fruitful farmland has been paved over for parking lots and new shopping centers. In addition bad farming practices have caused soil erosion, and as a result arable land has become scorched earth or desert. Palestine, the Holy Land itself, is a good example of barren landscapes because of the mismanagement of the land in the past. In the third point of the sermon one might deal with the "renewal of green pastures." The threat to the continuation of human life on this planet is a very real problem. Only recently has society become concerned with the danger to the greenery of the earth. The recognition of God's gift of creation should help human beings to recognize their own responsibility in caring for

God's creation. John was concerned in his own day with the rebellion of the forces of nature against the sin of Rome. In our day, we recognize the truth of John's relating man to his environment. Our sin is viewed in the shirking of our responsibility in keeping the pastures green.

Destruction of the Sea (8:8-9)

The second plague affects the sea—one third of the sea becomes blood—one third of the sea creatures die—one third of the boats are destroyed. Roman writers related the fact that the volcanic eruption on Santorini in the first century caused the sea around the island to turn red like blood. John has something similar in mind, when he says the seas will rebel against the sin of mankind.

Again in a timeless sense, John believes man's sin has affected the world about him. Our ecological sermon might emphasize then, what humans have done to the oceans. One thinks, of course, of the canisters of nerve gases that have been dropped into the oceans or the use of the seas as a garbage dump for nuclear wastes. It might not take us long to destroy the beautiful seas that took years to create. Our oceans cry out against our modern abuse much as John's seas screamed out against the sins of Rome.

Destruction of the Rivers (8:10-11)

The third plague falls upon the fresh water streams— and they become bitter. The bitterness is caused by a star called wormwood which falls into the fresh water. The background for this image probably is rooted in the eruption of the great volcano Vesuvius in A.D. 79. Roman records describe the hot lava hitting the fresh water streams and the ocean. John quite evidently has something like that in mind. In Revelation, the fresh water streams react to the great sin of Rome. The people who have tried to live without God now find that the water needed to sustain life has become foul.

Modern ecological interest reaches its highest intensity in reference to the preservation of the fresh water springs, rivers, and lakes of our world. Fresh water can no longer be taken for granted. Even in a country so blest with an abundance of fresh water, there is an emerging danger from pollution and lack of management of our precious resources. The close relationship between man and nature is even more evident today than in John's day. In that time the rivers and fresh water were reacting to what Rome had done to the Christian martyrs. In our day, we might reverse that pattern and call for Christians to react to what humans have done to the fresh water and streams.

These themes might be discussed in a sermon "He Leads Me Beside Still Water." Continuing with themes from Ps 23, the proclaimer could draw together under this title both trumpets two and three dealing with the pollution of the sea and the fresh water. The first point might stress the thought that "God leads us to the still waters." Life on this planet would be impossible without water. Travel and commerce from earliest history has depended upon the seas. As one reads the Bible, one is struck by the number of times God's love and concern is used in connection with giving a cup of cold water or leading his creatures to springs of cold water. Under the theme of "still water," the preacher might deal with man's responsibility to keep the water as God intended for it to be. John shrank back from seas that had become partially blood and fresh water that had become partly bitter. We today shrink back in horror from seas and fresh water that have become cesspools. The third theme might address "abiding" by the still waters. Future generations will be able to know the joys expressed in Psalm 23, only if present day men and women become concerned about the condition of the fresh water and seas of our earth. Pictures taken from outer space show earth to be a planet of water—blue-green colors predominate everywhere. How much longer will that be the case?

Destruction of the Heavenly Bodies (8:12)

The fourth trumpet blast brings a plague upon the heavenly bodies. They become instruments of God's judgment upon wicked Rome. The loss of one third of their light does not affect their intensity but in some way their duration. "A third of the day was kept from shining, and likewise a third of the night" (8:12). Thus one is confronted with the horror of darkness such as happened in Egypt (Exod 10:21-22). Yet in Revelation, God's restrained judgment is expressed in terms of the partial nature of the darkness.

The ecological theme of a modern sermon would continue here with emphasis upon man's pollution of the world above him. The celestial spaces are also becoming filled with man's garbage. From time to time, the danger alert is sounded to warn humans around the earth of the possibility of some spaceware falling back to earth. In addition the real threat of total darkness comes in the danger of intercontinental missiles armed with atomic warheads falling from the heavens. Man has within himself the power to destroy the whole world. Never has there been such a need to preach the theme of peace and peacemaking.

In a sermon, "The Quest for Peace," this basic need for peacemaking can be set forth. First, one might deal with the theme of peacemakers rather than peace talkers. So much emphasis is placed upon talking peace but little stress is involved in peace making efforts. Concrete action is needed to avoid the darkness that would come upon the earth if nuclear warfare should break out. If there is another war, destruction will rain down from the heavens in intercontinental missiles. Thus John's words, "a third of the day was kept from shining" becomes very realistic in our day. Secondly, the peace sermon should focus on the prince of peace, Jesus Christ. Peacemaking becomes somewhat nebulous for Christians unless it is related to the core of our faith. Christ has called upon us to be peacemakers in his name. War is outside God's purposes for mankind, for Christ came into the world to build a bridge between man and God. In the love of Christ, we in turn must build bridges to others. The name *pontifex maximus* is a name given to priests—meaning great bridge builder. The peacemaking quest is indeed one of building bridges. Thirdly, one might relate the theme of a peace which makes whole. God in Christ Jesus was seeking to reconcile the whole world unto himself. The whole purpose for the seven trumpets is to cause people to repent and find the peace which comes in relation to God. One-third destruction symbolizes God's mercy and love for the world and mankind. True peace must have as its ultimate goal the reconciliation of the whole universe. Revelation more than any other book shows us that picture of peace.

Destruction Brought by the Eagle (8:13)

The eagle is used extensively by John in Revelation to be a symbol of war or bad news. Earlier, we spoke of John's use of the Greek word *ouai* to mimic the screech of an eagle. In the interlude between the trumpets, the eagle appears to tell us that the last trumpets will be far worse than the first four. Three *ouai's* are pronounced in the interlude. In addition, each of the next trumpets will be called *ouai* trumpets.

Destruction of the Locusts (9:1–12)

The Fifth Trumpet introduces the first of John's monster beasts. Let us remember that in apocalyptic symbolism, monster beasts represent monster people. These monster beasts come up out of an abyss. Many ancient Greeks believed that volcanoes led from this world into the underworld. John has such a volcano structure in mind which leads to Hades or the underworld where the evil angels and other demonic forces are kept in prison. A star or more likely an angel descends with the key to this pit to permit these horrible forces to come forth upon the Roman Empire.

The forces of evil emerging are led by monster locusts. The ancient world lived in great dread of the periodic locust plagues which came upon their farmlands and fields. Nothing else could have threatened their very existence so greatly. Yet the locusts of Revelation are not normal locusts. They are the size of horses, with human faces, women's hair, and lions' teeth. In addition they have scorpion tales with which they inflict punishment and pain on those who have received the mark of the beast. The angel of the abyss, Abaddon or Apollyon, rules over them.

For John, these monster locusts symbolize the inner rot and decay of the Roman Empire. Gibbon related that one reason for the fall of Rome was its inner rot and decay. What better symbol could John have found to depict the inner moral sickness of the Roman enemy than monster locusts? It is interesting that in the parallel Fifth Bowl of Wrath (16:10–11) a plague of darkness settles over the throne of the beast. John needs a fearful monster beast to represent a fearful force—the corruptive influences of ancient Rome. In 18:3, John declares, "For all nations have drunk the wine of her impure passion." The period of *five* months also stands for judgment. This locust beast must have been encountered many times by those Christians living in the seven cities of Asia Minor.

The preacher of today must be very careful to understand John's symbolism here. There are many preachers who take these monster locusts literally and forecast their arrival at some date in the future. Some have even viewed John as predicting the development of the modern helicopter. However, there is excellent sermon material for a message concerning the moral darkness that is evident around our world. Dark and malignant forces are always at work in our midst and at times they emerge in persons such as Hitler or Stalin. Those who have eyes of faith know that if you live in darkness, you will eventually be destroyed by it. Roman depravity eventually brought about the fall of a once great society. In a timeless sense, the monster locusts of darkness are always eating away at the foundation of human society. Those who have been sealed with the mark of God never give in to this darkness and win victory over it. John says in the Fourth Gospel, "The light shines in the darkness, and the darkness has not overcome it" (John 1:5).

What better symbol than monster locusts can be found to symbolize the moral decay of our own world? John depicts these locusts eating away at the very foundations of human society. The text lends itself to speaking out on the need for Christians to be the salt of the earth. In many ways, the teachings of Jesus have been the agents of change needed to show the nations of the earth a better way. Dishonesty, corruption, and moral decay are always in abundance in our society. John was right in depicting these forces as "monster beasts." The teaching of Christ has preserved civilization and called human beings to a more noble life style. The text also shows us the need to be on guard against these "monster beasts" of decay. Sometimes their work is insidious, and the damage severe. It is much like termites at work in the foundation of one's home. Before they are discovered, serious structural damage can be carried out without our knowledge. John saw the inner rot and decay of the Roman world and realized it would one day lead to the destruction of that great empire. The history of mankind shows the rise and decay of great kingdoms. There are many destructive elements present in our own American society. If one has eyes of faith, he or she can see the monster locusts at work in our own age. Darkness is never far from the presence of light. It is only fitting for John to say that the locusts are ruled over by Apollyon, King of destruction. To offset the destructive forces of decay, believers must set forth Christian values to preserve the world.

Destruction of the Horsemen (9:13–21)

The sixth plague brings the invasion of barbarians riding monster beasts. Rome eventually fell to the barbarians from the east. Four angels bound at the Euphrates river which was the old eastern boundary of the Roman empire are set free to bring death on the earth. Beyond the Euphrates was the great Parthian nation which the Romans never were quite able to conquer. It is not surprising then that John has the two hundred million barbarians coming from the direction of the east. Throughout the Bible, barbarian hosts have been viewed as instruments of God's judgment. In 722 B.C., the nation of northern Israel fell to the Assyrians, and the ten tribes were led into captivity and completely disappeared from history. A few centuries later, in 587 B.C., the southern Jews were led into captivity for many decades. Both northern and southern prophets viewed these as actions of Yahweh. In a similar way, John describes the invasion of the barbarians as an instrument of God's wrath and judgment.

If one has eyes of faith, one may see the hand of God in all the moving forces of world history. Yet often in the face of divine judgment people will follow their old gods or immoral life style. After the destruction of Jerusalem, Jeremiah was amazed that the Israelites in Egypt started worshiping the local idols (Jer 44:15–25). In a similar way, John relates that even after the six trumpets, mankind did not give up its idolatrous worship nor evil practices (9:20–21). However, John wants us to see the ultimate victory of the forces of righteousness. Hitler boasted that Nazi Germany would last a thousand years—it barely made twelve years. A sermon incorporating this material should stress that these evil forces of corruption and evil never control the righteous, for those who walk in darkness will bring destruction upon themselves. One can be watchful for literal monster beasts to appear in the year 2000 and miss the destructive forces at work in today's world.

The popular tendency in dealing with Revelation's seven trumpets is to place them all at some time in the future. The timeless cyclical sequence of Revelation needs to be underlined. In our own age, the barbarians are never far removed from center stage. They represent the godless forces that are always prepared to degrade human life and insist on the mechanical rather than the personal. In John's day, the Romans made everyday life unbearable for Christians. However, in every age similar forces are at work. Secondly, the Gospel of Christ serves as a barrier against the barbaric forces of the world. A band of valiant Christians resisted all the power of Rome, and as a result many died and others were tormented. Yet the cause of Christ went forward. The Romans saw the conquered as human chattel—something to be used for their own purposes. Christianity teaches that every human being has worth and value before God. Thus Christianity spread rapidly among the slaves of Rome. Finally, we see in Revelation that the Lamb is ultimately victorious. The Romans who treated the Christians barbarically in turn fell to the barbarians from east of the Euphrates. The cross, the symbol of Roman barbarism, became the victorious symbol of the new Christian religion and stands forever as symbol of hope for the oppressed of the world.

Destruction Foretold in a Scroll (10:1-11)

There is an interlude in the action as John is told to take a scroll and eat it. This scroll, in contrast to the one in the hand of God, contains the last scenes of the Book of Revelation. Before John eats the scroll, he hears the seven thunders speak a message which he is not allowed to record. Then as he eats the scroll, it becomes sweet in his mouth but bitter in his stomach. This eating of the scroll symbolizes the message of judgment which the last scenes of Revelation depict coming upon the Romans. This will be "sweet in the mouth" of the Christians who have suffered at their hands. Yet when John sees the horror of those last days, the scroll becomes bitter in his stomach. A typical Christian living in one of the seven cities may have been quite happy to hear that Rome will be judged, for revenge is said to be sweet. Yet the full picture of judgment and upheaval may have "cooled down" even the most ardent feelings.

The passage concerning John eating the little scroll has several thoughts for preaching. Every proclaimer, like John, has a commission which has its sweet and bitter aspects. The word of God divides those who hear it proclaimed. Paul expressed it well in II Cor 2:15 and 16:

> For we are the aroma of Christ to God among those who are being saved and among those who are perishing, to one a fragrance from death to death, to the other a fragrance from life to life.

The Gospel by its very nature presses for a decision on the part of human beings. For those who have been sealed with the mark of the Lamb, the Gospel means good news and the promise of deliverance. For those who reject it, the Gospel brings judgment and condemnation of that which is evil. When John read the scroll which had been given him, the hope which it contained for persecuted Christians made its message sweet. However when he read of the judgment to come, its message became bitter. Like John, the modern proclaimer must present this dual message of the Gospel—allow its words to draw the lines of division. After John ate the scroll the angel gave the command: "You must again prophesy about many peoples and nations and tongues and kings" (10:11). The Gospel demands to be proclaimed—the preacher can do no other.

Destruction of the Outer Temple Courts (11:1-2)

John then is told to measure the inner courts of the temple but not the outer. In the Jewish temple in Jerusalem, the inner courts were reserved for the Israelites only. These courts were made up of the Court of Women, Court of the Israelites, Court of Priests, Holy Place and Holy of Holies. These inner Israelite courts were surrounded by the outer Gentile court. No Gentile was permitted to move from the outer courts into the inner on pain of death. The walls dividing the courts were real walls of division. John is giving here another message of hope for Christians. As new Israel, the Christians are measured. In symbolic language, the act of measuring represents protection. God's people will be protected throughout the coming Seven Bowls of Wrath. The outer courts, the non-believers, will receive the full impact of God's judgment. John makes use here of the number forty-two months, twelve hundred sixty days or three and a half years—all incomplete numbers. In Revelation, God works in fractions—there is always hope of repentance and restoration. The measuring scene undergirds God's people—no matter what persecution comes upon them—God will be with them.

In a sermon, "Walls of Division," one might deal with the radical changes brought about by the Christian Gospel over against the patterns of Jewish temple worship. First, the Jewish temple was made up of a series of walled off areas in which various segments of the population were segregated when they worshipped God. The Gentiles were allowed no further than the large outer court, for warning signs forbade them to come no closer. A wall separated the gentiles from the next court reserved for Jewish women. Females were considered unclean because of their menstrual blood and could come no closer to the presence of God. In this court, one also found unclean lepers as well as all children. A wall divided this Court of the Women from the Court of Israel—reserved for Jewish men and boys over the age of twelve. The men handed the sacrificial animals over a wooden rail which separated their court from that of the priests. The court of the Priests surrounded the sanctuary proper. Within this Court was the high altar of sacrifice. Finally, only one man, the high priest could enter the Holy of Holies to offer the blood of a goat once a year for the sins of the people. These various walls of division kept the different classes of people separate from God.

In Revelation, the true Christians are in the inner courts—the Holy Place and Holy of Holies. They have become priests before God. There are no divisions listed, for they stand as one before God. Paul expressed this truth in Galatians: "There is neither Jew nor Greek, there is neither slave nor free, there is neither male nor female; for you are all one in Christ Jesus" (Gal 3:28). The walls of division have been broken down. In Revelation, the only division is between believers and unbelievers. The outer courts are now inhabited by unbelievers. They are trampled down for forty-two months, an incomplete period of time. The true believers, all priests before God are secured by measuring. They now are before God without any respect of person or racial or sexual bias. It has taken the church a long time to learn this basic truth. In many of our modern day churches there are barriers that still exist among Christians. Women especially find it difficult to stand before God equal with men. Questions concerning service and ordination still are decided on the basis of sex. Sermons and Sunday School lessons frequently are filled with sexist language and phrases. True equality still has not been reached.

Destruction and Resuscitation of the Witnesses (11:3–14)

From the description given of the two witnesses, one would assume that they are Moses and Elijah. Like Elijah, the witnesses have the power to close the sky, and like Moses they have the authority to turn the waters into blood. In the Jewish synagogues, on each sabbath passages were read from the Law and the Prophets. Thus Moses and Elijah can symbolize here the Word of God. In many of the churches of Asia Minor, the Scripture had been taken from the Christians and destroyed. In symbolic form, Revelation is establishing the hope that God's Word will never be destroyed. At the very moment when the two witnesses are put to death, they come back to life and are taken to heaven. In the midst of persecution God will be with his people, and the promise is given that his Word will never be destroyed.

The two witnesses are symbolized by two lampstands or two olive trees. John borrows this symbolism from Zech 4:1–14 where a seven branched candlestick represents the eyes of God and the two living trees stand for Joshua and Zerubbabel. John replaces the seven branched candlestick with two lampstands and then identifies them with the two olive trees. As we have said, the two witnesses seem to be Moses and Elijah who bring the divine light of God found in the Law and Prophets. Throughout history, God's people have found hope in this promise in Revelation. Especially in times of persecution, Christians have rediscovered these statements about God's Word and have exercised hope. At the very moment we think the divine word is lost, it appears in new forms and manifestations. John's own word to the churches is such a new revelation.

"The Eternal Word of God" is a good title for a sermon on this passage. The Bible is not a book which needs to be defended or safeguarded. It has possessed the power to endure over the centuries. There have been many attempts to destroy the Bible because of its dramatic impact upon human lives. In the first century, the Romans would have been quite happy to have burned it or eradicated it completely. In John's symbolical presentation, this attempt to destroy the Word is represented in the murder of the two prophets in the street of the holy city. We have seen that Moses and Elijah symbolized the Word of God for many first century Christians. Yet, the Romans did not succeed in destroying the Word; the two prophets were brought back to life.

Thus, the Word of God is eternal, but this does not mean that it is to be worshipped. Bibleolatry is very dangerous in itself. The living word or prophetic word leads one beyond the Bible to a confrontation with the living Christ. The person of Christ stands above the word and is its judge because in the ultimate sense, he is the living Word of God become flesh. The Romans were not able to suppress the Word of God because it was alive and powerful. This same promise is available to Christians in every age to bring hope and comfort.

Destruction of the Destroyers (11:15–18)

The Seventh Trumpet brings with it a note of rejoicing in heaven. The twenty-four elders sing a hymn describing the reign of God.

> "The Kingdom of the world has become the kingdom of our Lord and of his Christ, and he shall reign for ever and ever" (11:15).

The music continues with a second hymn,

> "We give thanks to thee, Lord God Almighty, who art and who wast,
> that thou hast taken thy great power and begun to reign.
> The nations raged, but thy wrath came,
> and the time for the dead to be judged,
> for rewarding thy servants, thy prophets and saints,
> and those who fear thy name, both small and great,
> and for destroying the destroyers of the earth" (11:17–18).

Revelation 8:5—11:18

The elders give thanks because God has begun to reign. Unlike the kingdoms of this world, God's rule is filled with mercy and love. Rome had carried out its rule with a hard hand. God will carry out his rule with justice and truth. The rule of Caesar brought about fear and despair—death was never far away for those being oppressed. God's rule means life and hope for a new golden age. The elders sing of this reign with certainty even though it has not yet dawned with fullness.

The nations of the world oppose the rule of God. The divine concept of justice stands as an alien way to kings who have ruled by greed and dishonesty. The power to rule can be abused and distorted. Of course, those who have enjoyed the fruits of such power cry out when it is taken from them. Rage always results from thwarted political plans. Dictators especially resent the interruption of their schemes. John believes Rome's rule will be interrupted by the rule of God.

God's reign also means a time of rewards for the saints. The greatest of these is the gift of life or resurrection from the dead. John does not depict this reward in terms of crass materialism but rather as the saints participating in God's rule. Those who "fear the Lord" will share in the glorious kingdom that God has prepared for his own. The last chapters of Revelation will be given over to a description of this kingdom and what life will be like in it.

These hymns outline in essence the last acts of Revelation. God's forces are assured of victory even though the final battle has not yet taken place. Victory is a note that runs throughout this scene and really throughout this whole section of the Seven Trumpets. God is already at work judging the world. Even the forces of nature which he has created cry out against the sins of Rome. The forces of destruction and invading barbarians will not have ultimate control. In the midst of all these destructive forces God's people have been measured and given the promise of God's Word in the midst of their persecution. The Word of God has been safeguarded and will serve to guide the saints even in the midst of persecution—a truth symbolized by the death and resurrection of Moses and Elijah. Finally, a hymn of victory is sung by the twenty-four elders to celebrate God's rule over the earth. Throughout this section on the Seven Trumpets, emphasis has been placed on one third destruction of various aspects of the earth. The fraction represents incompleteness—it speaks of God's love and mercy for his people. The whole purpose of the trumpet plagues is to cause people to repent. In addition, the trumpets remind us of the three reasons for Rome's fall: (1) natural calamities—trumpets one-four; (2) inner rot and decay of the empire—trumpet five; and (3) the invasion of the barbarians—trumpet six. In spite of the judgment brought by these trumpets, mankind did not repent: "The rest of mankind, who were not killed by these plagues, did not repent of the works of their hands nor give up worshiping demons and idols of gold and silver and bronze and stone and wood, which cannot either see or hear or walk" (Rev 9:20).

Visions of Conflict
(Revelation 11:19—15:4)

In tableau fashion, this section of Revelation portrays the crucial struggle between good and evil down through history. A tableau depicts a striking dramatic scene with two or three prominent characters. Great emphasis is placed upon character studies and narrative motifs. Satan and his helpers presented as monster beasts stand over against the Lamb and his followers. The struggle goes on until one last battle between good and evil determines the ultimate outcome. As the action begins in 11:19, John beholds that the Holy of Holies of the heavenly Temple is open. One can look in and behold the Ark of the Covenant. This Ark played a very important role in Jewish history and symbolized God's presence with his people. The Israelites viewed the Ark as God's throne and a symbol of his presence among them. John makes use of the Ark to say that in the struggle with the forces of evil God will be with his people.

Throughout Revelation John makes much of the theme of hope for persecuted Christians. In the Visions of Conflict, the Ark becomes the central symbol of this hope. In Israelite history the Ark went before the people into battle; now it stands for the fact that God will lead his people against Satan and the demonic forces of Rome. Very few Israelites were ever in the Holy of Holies to view the Ark. Thus there is a note of mystery about it which also emerges in Revelation. As we prepare to view the Visions of Conflict depicting the struggle between good and evil, we are aware of the greater mystery that somehow is in it all, God will be present with his people. We are reminded of the covenants which he established with the children of Israel. He appeared to Abraham and inaugurated a covenant between himself and Abraham's descendants. He spoke to Moses at Mt. Sinai and gave to him the ten commandments. No Israelite could think of the Ark without also remembering the covenant promises of Yahweh. Early Christians hearing Revelation read aloud in the worship services would have also thought of God's covenants with his people when they heard the words concerning the Ark in 11:19. In the Apocalypse, even the gruesome picture of Satan and his two helper monster beasts can not block the view of the Ark. The Lamb and the 144,000, all true believers will wage war against the dragon with the Ark before them. The Christians in the seven churches viewed themselves as the new Israel. They saw God's promises and covenants being realized in the church. Israel of the flesh had turned its back upon Yahweh—now a new Israel in Jesus Christ had come into being.

The timeless cyclical nature of Revelation becomes very evident in the Visions of Conflict. Good preaching value can be gleaned from the theme of God's presence in the ongoing struggle between good and evil. The forces which John saw in conflict in the first century world are still in confrontation today. Evil and good are always on opposite sides. In Ephesians six, Paul warned the Christians to put on the whole armor of God to offset the wiles of Satan. In this ongoing struggle with evil, Christ will be with his people, and his promise of hope and security will abide forever. Christ defeated evil at the cross, and it will never again be a force to enslave men and women.

Satan Versus the Woman and Child (12:1-17)

There are three main characters in the First Vision—a woman, a child and a dragon. The action is also subdivided into three parts: (a) the woman, the child and the dragon (12:1-6); (b) Satan storms heaven (12:7-12); (c) Satan pursues the woman (12:13-17). The woman is obviously mother Israel, for John leaves us several clues to identify her. At the beginning of the scene, she is pregnant, is standing on the moon and has twelve stars on her head. The moon was very important in the cultic life of the Israelites. The major feast days were based on various phases of the moon, for indeed the Israelites used a lunar calendar. Every three years or so an extra month had to be added to bring it even with the solar calendar. As one reads the book of Psalms one becomes aware of the significance of the moon in the religious observances of the Jewish people. Moon watching stations were scattered across the land so that the word of the appearance of the new moon might be passed to Jerusalem.

The twelve stars on the woman's head symbolize the twelve tribes of Israel. Some have viewed them as representing the twelve signs of the zodiac. However, the Jewish background seems more directly applicable here. The twelve tribes play a great role throughout Revelation. As we have pointed out earlier, the twenty-four elders seem to represent the twelve tribes and the twelve disciples. In chapter twenty-one, when John beholds the new Jerusalem, the names of the twelve tribes appear upon the twelve gates of the city. In chapter seven, the new Israel is made up of twelve thousand from each of the twelve tribes.

The woman is clothed in the sun, a resplendent dress which symbolizes the great messianic promises of the OT. The woman is ready to give birth to a child—the Messiah. Many Jews of the NT period were living in the expectation of the birth of the Messiah. However, several different messianic expectations from warrior Messiah to priest Messiah existed in the first century. As the war with Rome approached in A.D. 70, messianic expectations flourished. However, John wants us to see that the woman's child is Jesus Christ the long awaited Messiah. The First Vision gives to mother Israel all the splendor and glory as might befit the mother of the Messiah.

The second character in the Vision is the person of Satan. He is depicted as a red sea dragon with seven heads and ten horns. Throughout the OT, the Israelites feared the sea and especially the large sea monsters like Behemoth, Leviathan, and Rahab (Job 7:12; Ps 74:14; 89:10; Isa 27:1). Even the early creation story has God doing battle with the "Tohuwabohu," the swirling mass of black water from whence he created the dry land. The seven heads of the dragon represent his claims to divinity. The ten horns symbolize his complete power in this age. In general, apocalyptic literature holds a two-sided view of history: the present age completely under the power of evil and the age to come which will bring the fulfillment of God's promises to his people. The ten horns are also mentioned in reference to the beast of Dan 7:7. The seven crowns denote the princely power of the dragon. The red color stands for the murderous activity of Satan in the death of the Christian martyrs. However, we are reminded that Satan's power is incomplete for he has the power to cast only one third of the stars to earth. In Revelation, Satan is never presented as an equal to God since his power is always limited and his defeat is surely imminent.

The figure of the baby is obviously the new born Messiah. We are told that Satan stands nearby ready to devour the baby. The Messiah stands over against the dragon as the herald of God's promises to his people. In a sermon called simply "The Woman, Child, and the Dragon," the preacher might deal with the following points: (1) John makes no attempt to give us a history of the Messiah or even a life of Jesus as Messiah. Rather the emphasis is placed upon the complete victory of the Messiah over Satan on earth as well as heaven. (2) Satan is foiled in his attempts to destroy the child, for the Messiah is under the protection of God. Great stress is placed upon the fact that the birth of the Messiah brought the conflict between good and evil to a head. Satan lost his claim to princely power and divinity. (3) The struggle between good and evil involves Christians of all ages.

The baby is born and is caught up to heaven. Satan storms heaven to destroy the Messiah and is defeated by Michael and his angels. Michael was viewed as the patron angel of Israel and the leader of the angelic host against any enemy of God (Dan 10:21; 12:1). Satan's defeat is also complete in heaven. He is thrown back down to earth where in his final days he will war against the woman and her descendants. One can sense here that the Messiah is destined to bring about the final victory over Satan. Though that victory has not yet been won, it is already assured. In reaction to that assurance, the heavenly choir breaks out into a hymn:

> "Now the salvation and the power
>   and the kingdom of our God
>   and the authority of his Christ have come,
> for the accuser of our brethren has been thrown down,
>   who accuses them day and night before our God.
> And they have conquered him by the blood of the Lamb
>   and by the word of their testimony,
> for they loved not their lives even unto death.
> Rejoice then, O heaven and you that dwell therein!
> But woe to you, O earth and sea,
>   for the devil has come down to you
> in great wrath,
>   because he knows that his time is short!" (12:10–12).

The hymn gives great hope to the church of the final destruction of evil in the world. A sermon drawn from the hymn might emphasize the following points: (a) salvation has come, (b) the accuser of the brethren has been thrown down, (c) rejoice then, O heaven. The ultimate source of the victory resides in the blood of the Lamb. God's redemptive work in the cross has brought about the ultimate defeat of Satan. The power of sin has become naught because of the cross. The testimony of the martyrs emerges as the channel through which this victory is proclaimed. The celebration of victory rests upon the redemptive work of the Lamb and the testimony of the martyrs.

The woman now becomes new Israel or the Church. Satan, having been cast down from heaven pursues the woman and her descendants. The latter word brings the Christians of the seven churches into the picture. What has just been depicted in story form gives the rationale of the destructive wave of evil which those Christians were experiencing in the first century. Satan was actively involved in the severe Roman persecution of the believers. Yet within the narrative there is also a message of hope and security for believers. In the struggle with Satan, God protects the woman and provides her a safe place in the desert. John may have had in mind the flight of the Jerusalem church to Pella during the Roman-Jewish war of A.D. 70. The wings of an eagle given to the woman symbolize this message of hope (Deut 32:11; Isa 40:31).

The struggle with Satan will be a difficult one. Yet the Christians of Asia Minor are convinced that God will keep them safe "in his hand." In a timeless sense, that message also needs to be declared by the preacher to his people. At times in the modern world, it seems as if evil is in control. The ultimate message of Revelation is that the Lamb will rule eternally–not Caesar nor Satan.

Satan's Ally: The Sea Beast (13:1–10)

The Second Vision features the chief ally of Satan—the beast from the sea. From John's point of view, the best example of Satan's anger could be seen in the evil destructive influences of Rome. Hence the beast from the sea is a symbol of corrupt political power as manifested in the Roman empire.

The close relationship between this beast and Satan is evident in the similarities of their forms. For example, both beasts have seven heads, ten horns and are grotesque in form. The one distinctive difference is that the beast has ten crowns—one on each horn whereas the Satan has seven. The ten crowns probably represent the ten Parthian kings that are brought together for the last battle between good and evil in 19:19ff. The blasphemous names are the divine titles given to Caesar by the ten kings.

John's further description of the beast pinpoints its political markings. John takes the symbols of the three most powerful nations of his day—Medea, Persia and Rome and weaves together the horrible political monster beast. The bear's feet represent Medea, the leopard—Persia, and the lion—Rome. The conglomerate figure is also a combination of the first three beasts of Daniel. The seven heads of the beast stand for the seven Caesars from the time of Christ's crucifixion to the period of Revelation:

Tiberius	— A.D. 14–37
Caligula	— A.D. 37–41
Claudius	— A.D. 41–54
Nero	— A.D. 54–68
Vespasian	— A.D. 69–79
Titus	— A.D. 79–81
Domitian	— A.D. 81–96

John relates that one head seems to have a mortal wound which has been healed. This is quite likely a reference to the Nero redivivus myth current at the time. Nero had not really been slain but would return and rule once again over the Roman empire. The great authority of Satan himself is given to this political beast. John wants to make it quite clear that anyone worshiping this political beast—Rome—is in reality worshiping Satan. Statues of Caesar Domitian were set up all over Asia Minor. One of the largest ever found was at Ephesus. The blasphemy connected with the worship of the political beast was the use of the phrase, "Caesar is Lord." The early confession of the Christian church had been "Jesus is Lord." Sometimes those Christians being forced to worship Caesar's statue were also forced to curse the name of

Christ. "And they worshiped the beast, saying, 'Who is like the beast, and who can fight against it?' " (13:4). We are told that all will worship the beast except those whose names are written in the Book of Life. True Christians will never give in to Caesar worship. Some believers, less than true, might bow down to Caesar's statue in order to buy food for their families. Christians must be steadfast throughout the persecution and not try to escape the pain and the death. The admonition to the saints reads:

> If any one is to be taken captive,
>   to captivity he goes;
> if any one slays with the sword
>   with the sword must he be slain (13:10).

The political beast reminds us that evil destructive forces can be manifested in national, state, and local governments. There is a real danger of the church becoming overly identified with the state. In Romans thirteen, Paul could praise the Roman empire and call upon Christians to obey it. In A.D. 56 or 57 when Paul wrote the passage, Rome had not brought any major persecutions on the Christians. Nero would change all of that. By the time of John's writing Revelation thirteen, Rome had become the beast. In considering the Christian's relationship to the state, one must always ponder Romans thirteen over against Revelation thirteen. Jesus once declared that Roman money with Caesar's face on it belonged to Rome. However, he also taught that there was a realm which belonged to God. Many German Christians did little to resist Hitler's use of the state church in Germany during World War II. They heard only the words of Paul in Romans thirteen—to obey the government. Other Christians resisted even to death because they realized that Hitler might well be the beast of Revelation thirteen. Some of those who gave in to Hitler were the very ones expecting a literal seven headed beast to appear from the sea in A.D. 2000 and missed the one in 1936.

The futurists have abused this passage concerning the beast from the sea. Even today many books are on the shelves of bookstores purporting to tell us who this beast will be in A.D. 1988 or A.D. 2025. The preacher must stress relating the meaning of this passage to the first century Christians of

Asia Minor in the context of Caesar worship. From that point, he or she might stress the timeless message that evil often comes in the guise of political power. How does one control the earth through the use of political force? If one really wants to try to control the minds of people, political power is the best way to do it. Persons like Hitler demonstrate what evil can do when it controls the state. At times we have seen in our own country how political power can be abused, bringing with it destructive forces. A sermon here should stress the need for Christians to get involved in politics and safe guard our system of government. At the same time, emphasis should also be placed on the separation of church and state. Channels of communication should be kept open but identities kept separate. One might call this sermon "The Christian Standing between Romans Thirteen and Revelation Thirteen." The following points should be emphasized: (1) political power and evil—the beast (13:1-4), (2) political power and Christians—the struggle (13:10), and (3) political power redeemed—the hope (12:17).

Satan's Ally: The Land Beast (13:11-18)

Satan's second ally is the beast from the land. This beast comes in the guise of the Lamb. In other words it is a religious beast. With one exception the beast from the land mimics the appearance of the Lamb—Jesus Christ. The only major difference is that the second beast has two horns instead of seven. Like the first beast, it has the power and authority of the dragon, Satan. However, its major task is to call people to bow down and worship the first beast. In all of the cities of Asia Minor under Domitian there was a group of priests (twelve in number) who were responsible for carrying out Caesar worship. They were given the task of erecting the statues of Domitian in the major Roman cities. They were also in charge of the rules and regulations governing such worship in the local communities. John asserts, "Also it causes all, both small and great, both rich and poor, both free and slave, to be marked on the right hand or the forehead" (13:16). This marking could be a reference to the practice in some ancient religions of the adherents branding themselves with the image of a god. Ptolemy Philadelphus forced some Alexandrian Jews to be branded with the mark of Dionysus (3 Macc 2:29). Perhaps John has in mind the use of Roman coinage with the head of Caesar inscribed upon it. It is possible that Caesar worship itself may have involved such a branding on the forehead or back of the hand. The bases of many ancient statues have been found to be hollow in order to permit the priests of a particular deity to enter them and speak through that statue. It may have been that Caesar worship involved such practices. "It works great signs, even making fire come down from heaven to earth in the sight of men" (13:13). Ancient priests were well skilled in magical tricks and incorporated these into Caesar worship as well. The major purpose of the second beast is to cause the inhabitants of the world to worship the first beast—the power of Rome.

The number of this beast is 666. In apocalyptic literature six is often the code number for the enemy. Several attempts have been made to relate a proper name to these code numbers. The best attempt seems to be to take the Hebrew letters for Nero Caesar—N = 50, R = 200, O = 6, N = 50 and K = 100, S = 60, and R = 200. Several other attempts have been made to bring in the name of Trajan, or such terms as Caesar of Rome or even primal chaos. However, from what has been said about the first beast earlier in chapter thirteen, one can suppose that Caesar Nero is a prime candidate. Many early Christians believed that Nero had returned in the form of Domitian. Never since the time of Nero had there been so much persecution of the Christians.

The second beast contains the message of political power gone wild—turned into a religion. In the first century, the Caesar cult became a religion numbered with the other major religions of the empire. In every Roman colony, the temple to Roma or the Caesar was always the most impressive one. Throughout world history evil has often expressed itself in political garb and been enshrined in temples. One need only to view the old propaganda films of Nazi Germany to realize the religious overtones of the movement. Those who proclaimed "Heil, Hitler" around the great bonfires were doing so out of religious passion. The state can become the object of worship as much as an idol or deity. Even though they claim to be atheistic, card carrying communists are very religious in their cause.

In the United States Americanism and Christianity often are confused. Many foreigners visiting our churches are often surprised to see the large number of American flags displayed. At times in regions of the United States, the local church reflects more the cultural values of the region rather than those of Christ. "The Religious Beast" serves as a good title for a sermon dealing with some of the dangers of the worship of political power rather than Christ. The points of the sermon could be: (1) the religious beast and his worship (13:11–14), (2) the religious beast and his mark (13:16), and (3) the religious beast and Christ (14:1).

There has also been great speculation about the so-called mark of the Beast. John speaks of a mark on the back of the hand or the forehead. Point two of the sermon needs to deal forthrightly with the historical background to avoid such speculation as social security cards, plastic money cards as being the mark of the beast. Futurists speak of a gigantic computer to be built in Belgium which will bring about a one world currency. Such speculation robs Revelation of its timeless meaning rooted in history. Political power can be used of evil and be turned into a worship service. In this sermon, the preacher also needs to deal forthrightly with the number of the religious beast—666—in the setting of Caesar worship of the first century. Probably no other number is so often abused by the futurists. Each generation of young Christians has its own candidate. One recent name circulating among the college crowd is Ronald Wilson Reagan because he has six letters in each of his names. Widows have even been frightened by receiving social security checks with the numbers 666 in their serial numbers. Such speculation needs to be put to rest with a good historical introduction to Caesar worship.

Satan Versus the Lamb (14:1–5)

In the Fourth Vision, the side of the righteous comes into focus. We have encountered the forces of evil led by Satan and his two monster beasts. Now we behold the Lamb on Mt. Sion with the 144,000 faithful. In the struggle with Satan, the Lamb will lead the righteous. There is no reason for believers to stand in fear of Satan and his monster allies. The 144,000 must be viewed over against the 144,000 of chapter seven.

They represent the whole body of true believers. These faithful ones have the seal of God upon their foreheads. Thus they stand in stark contrast to the persons bearing the mark of the beast. These believers have fought the forces of evil and have won the battle with them. They have earned the right to sing a new song before God's heavenly throne room.

The description of these 144,000 faithful furnished by John seems rather strange to modern ears:

> "It is these who have not defiled themselves with women, for they are chaste; it is these who follow the Lamb wherever he goes; these have been redeemed from mankind as first fruits for God and the Lamb, and in their mouth no lie was found, for they are spotless (14:4–5).

The faithful are called "chaste" because they have not involved themselves in the Caesar cult nor in some of the local fertility cults which practiced sacred prostitution. So often in the OT, marriage motifs are used to describe Israel's relationship to God. When Israel turned its back upon Yahweh, the prophets used words like "adultery" or "immorality" to describe the action (see Hosea). The phrase "no lie was found in their mouth" could refer to the "lies" involved in the confession of Caesar as Lord.

It may also be that John viewed the faithful as a great army led by the Lamb. In Deut 23:9–10 careful directions are given for those who will serve in the army of God: "When you go forth against your enemies and are in camp, then you shall keep yourself from every evil thing" (23:9). Here in Revelation, the believers are viewed as a holy army led by the Lamb and marching against the forces of evil. The asceticism of the army is to be taken in a moral context. These soldiers have avoided the pollution of the Caesar cults and the local fertility cults. Only such dedicated soldiers could overcome and defeat Satan and his followers.

This passage lends itself to preaching on the discipline needed to practice the Christian life style. Just as many Americans have allowed themselves to get "out of shape" physically, many Christians have also gotten "out of shape" spiritually. Across the country, more and more people are becoming involved in physical fitness as jogging becomes a national past-time. In the spiritual realm, some Christians have known the power of a disciplined Christian life style. Contemplation has become a lost art among Christians as well as the practices of fasting and an organized devotional life. In the struggle with evil, the church needs the strongest Christians necessary. John saw the 144,000 overcoming evil because of their commitment to the cause and their rigid separation from the evil forces of their time. We might call this sermon, "Soldiers of Christ." The basic points could be, (1) the spiritual discipline of the Christian soldier (14:4a–5), (2) the focus of the Christian soldier (14:3), and (3) the task of the Christian soldier (14:4b).

The reward for such commitment is fellowship with the Lamb and participation in the worship of heaven. A message of hope radiates throughout the whole picture. No force can withstand the Lamb and his followers. No matter what devious means the forces of evil may use, the righteous message of the Lamb and his followers will never be overcome.

Satan's Allies Warned (14:6–13)

Before the Fifth Vision arrives, three angels appear with three important messages for Satan's allies. In view of the ultimate victory of the Lamb, the first angel announces: "Fear God and give him glory, for the hour of his judgment has come; and worship him who made heaven and earth, the sea and the fountains of water" (14:7). God is established as the creator of all persons in the world. Hence the call is for all people to bow down and worship him. In view of God's judgment, the mood is here not one of gloom and doom. Rather, the inhabitants respond in worship of the one who stands for justice and mercy. This message is referred to as "glad tidings," not something to be dreaded. There is a great need for the judgment of God to be presented in positive words rather than negative. Some preachers are always proclaiming what a person is "saved from" rather than what one is "saved to." It is much easier to paint the fires of hell rather than God's reign of justice and mercy upon the earth.

The second angel announces the destruction of Babylon. Throughout Revelation, Babylon has been a code name for Rome. "Fallen, fallen is Babylon the great, she who made all nations drink the wine of her impure passion" (14:8). Rome's influence had spread across the Mediterranean world. This oracle of woe comes directly from the Old Testament passages of Isa 21:9 and Jer 50:2. Rome had seduced the nations of the world to partake of her immorality. Caesar worship had been established in many of the great cities of the empire. Even the philosophers of Rome often spoke out against the decadent life style which characterized the Roman empire. In chapters seventeen through nineteen, John will spell out the details of Rome's punishment and destruction. With an assurance which has characterized his writing, John can speak of the fall of Rome as if it had already happened.

The third angel presents a warning to anyone who might be contemplating participating in the Caesar cult. In fact this warning is one of the strongest in the whole book.

> "And the smoke of their torment goes up for ever and ever; and they have no rest, day or night, these worshipers of the beast and its image, and whoever receives the mark of its name" (14:11).

In such a period of dire persecution, it was important to warn the faithful to resist Caesar worship. Persecution is often a test which weeds out the true Christians from those loosely connected to the churches. To escape a few moments of persecution, a follower might be willing to curse the name of Christ—especially to buy food for his family. John would have all those in the churches to realize that a few moments of relief gained by worshiping Caesar would be insignificant in comparison to the resulting eternity of punishment.

The interlude concludes with a call for the endurance of the saints and a blessing bestowed upon those "who die in the Lord henceforth" (14:12-13). In the midst of persecution, true Christians must be willing to suffer and even die for the cause of Christ. John needed to hold before the faithful the great rewards the martyrs were enjoying and would enjoy in the presence of God's throne. Throughout Revelation great emphasis has been placed on the martyrs. In the early church many believed that martyrs at death went directly to be before God without having to wait in their graves until the resurrection day.

A sermon developed around the messages of the three angels should stress the narrow road that leads into the kingdom and be entitled, "Narrow is the Way." (1) It is a road that brings the joy of worshiping a God of love. The pilgrimage with God must always be viewed first of all as a joyous experience. (2) Yet in the midst of joy, the Christian must at times endure the pain of trial and persecution. Punishment and reward are always peripheral matters—the perimeters of the pilgrimage. Preachers of the past have either overemphasized the rewards, making Christianity into a "sweet by and by" kind of faith or a "hell fire and damnation" religion. The joy of the march and the comfort of hope should always be on central stage. (3) The way has been travelled by Christ and his footsteps are our guide. Though the way is difficult, we are never alone.

Satan Versus the Son of Man (14:14–16)

The followers of Christ can be assured that the judgment of God will be a solace for the righteous. Satan and his helpers: the political beast and the religious beast seem to be in control of things. Yet Revelation gives to the saints the assurance that the Lamb will be their leader and that God's judgment will establish righteousness upon the earth. John makes use of a harvest motif: first a harvest of wheat and then a harvest of grapes. The harvest and vintage motifs are found extensively throughout the Bible. In Joel 3:13, we read,

> Put in the sickle,
>   for the harvest is ripe.
> Go in, tread,
>   for the wine press is full.
> The vats overflow,
>   for their wickedness is great.

The end of the world is often termed the harvest (Mark 4:29; Jer 51:33; Hos 6:11).

The judgment of the Son of man is proleptic here. It is announced but will not actually be described until chapters nineteen through twenty-one. The focus of judgment is the temple of God. At the beginning of the Visions of Conflict, the Holy of Holies was open so that one might see the Ark of the covenant. Now near the end of these Visions, judgment emanates from the temple. God will not leave his people alone in their hour of trial. For the righteous, the judgment of God has no element of fear. The same Son of man figure who stood in the midst of the lampstands (chapter 1) is the same who brings God's judgment upon the world. God's concern for his creation is evident in the fact that he will not leave it in the control of destructive forces. Evil will be vanquished and destroyed from the face of the earth.

Revelation, like Job of the OT, does not really provide an answer to why bad things happen to good people. Yet an assurance is given much like the message of Job that even in difficulty God is still there. However, Revelation goes a step further and speaks of the justice of God prevailing over the forces of evil. It must have been difficult for Christians in Ephesus or Thyatira to keep their faith firm in the promises of God. The seven headed beast of Rome must have always been easier to visualize than the Son of man with his sickle. Anywhere one traveled in the seven cities one saw signs of the power of Rome. Roman soldiers were always near and the threat of arrest was never far away. Yet the faithful were also never far from the Lamb with seven eyes and seven horns and his promises of victory. These truths could be expressed in a sermon called, "Why Bad Things Happen to Good People": (1) the incomplete answer (Job 21:7), (2) the basic hope—God is there (Job 42:2), and (3) the justice of God will prevail (Rev 14:16).

Satan's Allies Judged (14:17-20)

John places more emphasis upon the harvest of grapes than the harvest of grain. The juice of the grapes becomes for him a graphic symbol of the blood of the hated Romans flowing in the city streets. The measure of the blood is rather grotesque, "as high as a horse's bridle, for one thousand six hundred stadia" (14:20). Such an exaggerated measurement seems to have been typical of Jewish literature in referring to the judgment of God. Some have viewed the sixteen hundred stadia as a square of forty—the typical period of punishment in Israelite history (Num 14:33; Deut 25:3). In I Enoch, we find the words, "The horse shall walk up to the breast in the blood of sinners, and the chariot shall be submerged to its height" (I Enoch 100:1-2). It is obvious that Jewish hyperbole is at work here. John was making use of a standard apocalyptic picture of God's final judgment.

In Greek tragic drama, the final resolution of the action

was always brought about by Zeus or some other god who would be lifted from the upper stage building by means of the *deus ex machina* to the lower stage. This god brought the solution to the problems that had come to view during the drama. A decisive act of the gods ended the action. In a similar way the evil destructive forces of Revelation are dealt a final definitive blow. John had to deal seriously with the presence of evil in the world. He could have contended himself to describe the beauty of paradise and the reward of the faithful. Yet he desired to paint a scene of graphic destruction of evil. Isaiah also depicted God as a warring king who would trample the nations opposing Israel (63:1–6).

Perhaps we need a graphic presentation like John's to present the truth of evil's ultimate defeat. In Greek drama, the actors wore masks so that the mood of the play could be perceived in the frowns and smiles inscribed on their faces. Sometimes forces like judgment and defeat need to be expressed in technicolor—in symbols that even the dullest reader might comprehend. In comic books temptation is often depicted by means of a little devil with pitchfork flying on one side of the character's head. On the other side an angel with fluttering wings represents the right or moral way. Not even a child could miss the obvious choice set before the comic book character. No one viewing this Vision can miss what John is saying about God's judgment. Perhaps there is a message here for all preachers to realize the importance of the rich use of symbolism in preaching.

A sermon on this Vision might be called "Right must Prevail." (1) John uses the symbolical language of the reaper to portray God as the judge of the world. (2) The wrath of God represents his divine righteousness at work in the world. (3) The flow of blood stands for the finality of God's judgment. (4) The sixteen hundred stadia symbolizes the completeness of God's judgment.

Satan's Defeat Celebrated (15:1–4)

As happens so often in Revelation, a major section comes to an end with singing and worship in heaven. The martyrs stand by the Sea of Glass and join in the song of Moses and of the Lamb:

"Great and wonderful are thy deeds,
O Lord God the Almighty!
Just and true are thy ways,
O King of the ages!
Who shall not fear and glorify thy name, O Lord?
For thou alone art holy.
All nations shall come and worship thee,
for thy judgments have been revealed" (15:3–4).

This final Vision concludes one section of Revelation and introduces us to the next—the Bowls of Wrath. As the martyrs sing the new song of Moses, we can see the seven angels with the last plagues of God appear in the background. These martyrs sing of the power and majesty of God. The Song of Moses relates back to the hymn that Israel sang by the Red Sea after their deliverance by Yahweh (Exod 15:1–2), and the hymn recited by Moses at the end of his life (Deut 32:1–2). The first two verses remind us clearly of Exodus 15 and the final verses bring to mind Exodus 32.

The final Vision of Conflict confronts us with a sermon concerning "The God who Acts." (1) Throughout the OT the Israelites celebrated the acts of God in their pilgrimage with him. Their major festivals recalled ways in which God had actively come to the aid to deliver them. Their chief festival of Passover celebrated the deliverance of Israel through the Red Sea. (2) In fact at times, Judaism has seemed to be a religion of the past and the future, looking to God's past acts on behalf of his people and awaiting the coming Messiah and his reign. (3) John also in the new song of Moses celebrates a God who is acting in his world. He is not just a God of the past but also active in the present. He is now redeeming his people and watching over his persecuted followers. Soon all the world will be aware of his concern for his people.

The Visions of Conflict have presented in realistic character sketches the struggle between good and evil. That action has been played out on the stage in front of the opened Holy of Holies with its Ark of the Covenant clearly manifested. Thus we are aware from the beginning that God will be with his faithful even in the direct conflict with Satan and his two monster helpers. These scenes so rich in symbolism highlight the Lamb as the true guide and leader of the righteous. Who can resist his power? How can anyone doubt his ultimate victory?

Visions of Wrath
(Revelation 15:5—16:21)

The seven angels bearing the seven bowls of God's wrath emerge from the heavenly Temple and prepare to pour plagues out on the face of the earth. The cyclical action which has marked Revelation up to this point begins to move more strongly forward in a spiral pattern. John is describing God's final judgment upon the earth. With the fall of Rome, the Seer feels that the end of the age will come quickly, and that God will pour out his judgment upon the world. Up to this point, God's judgment has been restrained in order to allow his mercy to be perceived by mankind. The Seven Trumpets brought only one third destruction, but now the Seven Bowls will intensify everything that happened with the blowing of the Seven Trumpets.

In the Visions of Conflict, the temple stood open revealing the Holy of Holies. With the pouring out of the Seven Bowls, the temple is filled with the smoke of the glory of God. No one can enter into the temple nor carry out the sacrifices and rituals. The closed temple symbolizes the final acts of God's judgment. In addition, the Sea of Glass in the heavenly scene becomes mingled with fire. This fiery symbol tells us that these seven plagues ". . . are the last, for with them the wrath of God is ended" (15:1).

The seven angels bearing the plagues are dressed like priests prepared to do service in God's temple. They are dressed in white with gold bands around their chests. The white color represents the purity of their task while the golden girdles about their chests speak of the worth and value of their work. These angels have the mission of carrying out God's purposes and plans. Throughout Revelation, angels have played a very significant role. On many occasions, they have been in charge of the various elements of the earth: wind, fire, or water. Their sole duty seems to be the fulfillment of God's will. Now seven angels are singled out to carry out God's final judgment upon mankind.

The pure bright linen of the angels stands in stark contrast to the filthy clothing of the Romans. On several occasions, John has spoken of the need to refrain from wearing unclean garments (3:4). The Romans' clothing was soiled with the blood of the martyrs and with the immorality that characterized the empire. In Rev 6:11, the martyrs under the altar in heaven were given white robes to put on. During their sojourn on earth, they had not soiled their garments with Caesar worship and immoral fertility cults. In 19:14, the armies that return with Christ are robed in "fine linen, white and pure." God stands as holy and pure and his judgments are righteous.

The Seven Bowl judgments come very quickly. There are no interludes in this section of Revelation, for there will be no more delay. God gave the Romans many opportunities to repent, but they responded with blasphemies and curses. The judgments brought by the Seven Trumpets confronted them with the fact that the universe itself was turning its back upon them. Now the action moves swiftly as the bowl plagues fall upon those bearing the mark of the Roman beast. Each plague will be complete within itself and intensify the parallel trumpet plague. As we have said earlier, both trumpet and bowl plagues bear a direct relation to the ten Egyptian plagues of Moses' time.

Plague on Mankind (16:2)

The First Bowl is poured out upon the earth and vile sores break out on those bearing the mark of the beast. The intensity of the plagues is marked by the fact that the very first one comes upon mankind. In the trumpet plagues, the first did not come upon man until plague number five. With the First Bowl plague, ulcerous sores break out on those bearing the mark of the beast—those who have participated in Caesar worship. The First Trumpet plague affected one third of the greenery of the earth. In contrast, the First Bowl goes beyond the world of nature to man, himself. It also reminds us very much of the sixth Egyptian plague (Exod 9:8–12). There Moses and Aaron cast ashes into the air and brought about boils and sores upon the people and their beasts. The same word used here in Revelation to describe the ulcerous sores is also employed in Luke to describe the poor beggar at Lazarus' gate and in the Greek OT to portray the plight of Job.

It is interesting that each plague in Revelation is designed to fit the particular sin of the Romans involved. The author of the Wisdom of Solomon reflects upon the plagues of Egypt and declares that these judgments came so "that they might learn that one is punished by the very things by which he sins" (11:15–16). One can almost visualize with John the mark of the Beast upon human bodies slowly turning into ulcerous sores. Those who surrendered their bodies to Caesar would receive a fitting judgment in their bodies. The sores themselves would testify to the fact that these persons were enslaved by Caesar.

One can observe in life that persons often bring upon themselves judgment that is very fitting for the sin. People who live a life of crime depending upon the power of a gun often end up as a victim of a gun. Others may lead a life punctuated by hatred and anger which eventually may consume them. The writer James expressed it well, "Each person is tempted when he is lured and enticed by his own desire. Then desire when it has conceived gives birth to sins; and sin when it is full grown brings forth death" (1:14–15). Those who surrendered their bodies to Caesar worship brought upon themselves the ulcerous sores of their punishment. These truths can be developed in a sermon called "Sin Full Grown." The following points might be set forth from James and Revelation: (1) personal desire gives birth to sin (James 1:14), (2) judgment is related to sin (Rev 16:2), and (3) full grown sin brings death (James 1:15).

Plague on the Sea (16:3)

The Second Bowl is poured out upon the sea, and immediately it becomes like the blood of a dead person. In Trumpet Two, one third of the sea became blood. Now in Bowl Two it is even more intensified as all the sea turns into blood—the blood of a dead person. John subdivides the first Egyptian plague on the Nile into two plagues—one on the sea and one on the fresh waters (Bowls Two and Three). The Roman empire depended upon the seas to transport its influences around the Mediterranean Sea. Now that Sea has become the black coagulated blood of a dead person, and all life in the sea perishes.

In Paul's day, Rome's great accomplishments of travel and transportation were seen as favorable to the growth of Christianity. Paul traveled on Roman roads to the distant points of the Empire in order to spread the Gospel. The Roman postal system enabled him to write back his epistles to newly founded churches. In addition, the conquests of Rome introduced one language—Greek—across the Mediterranean world which enabled Paul to be heard and understood on his many journeys. By A.D. 95, Roman power had become corrupt and an obvious threat to Christianity. The deification of Caesar was a real and present danger to a monotheistic faith. Thus John saw even the roads of Rome, its sea routes and postal system as threats to Christianity. The ships that crossed the seas brought the "wine of her immorality."

> "Thy merchants were the great men of the earth,
> and all nations were deceived by thy sorcery.
> And in her was found the blood of prophets and of saints,
> and of all who have been slain on earth" (18:23–24).

It is very fitting that such a corrupt power as Rome should see the very seas around it turn black with decayed blood. The sea mirrored the moral condition of the empire.

A good sermon title here might be "The Seas of Revelation." The preacher might contrast the Sea of Glass and the Sea of Death. (1) In chapters four and five the sea was depicted as calm, reflecting the perfect harmony of the worship in God's heavenly throne room. That sea mirrored the joy and celebration of the victorious Christian martyrs. (2) In stark contrast, the sea of death reflects the gaudy, decaying image of Rome. The empire would drown in the sewer of its own iniquities and perverted designs. Sometimes inner decay is more dangerous than outer attack. (3) We often hear Christians express a fear of Satan's attack but in reality a far greater danger exists from a sea of our inner selfish desires and wants.

Plague on the Rivers (16:4–7)

The Third Bowl is poured out upon the fresh waters and streams—they also become blood. In the Third Trumpet plague, one-third of the waters became bitter because of the wormwood which fell into them. The theme of "befitting judgment" is expressed very clearly by the angel of the water.

> "Just art thou in these thy judgments,
> thou who art and wast, O Holy One.

For men have shed the blood of saints and prophets,
and thou hast given them blood to drink.
It is their due!" (16:5b–6).

These verses in Revelation are almost in direct parallel with Wisdom 11:5–6 which was quoted earlier in this section.

It is only fitting that the angel in charge of the altar is designated to pronounce the second statement (16:7) concerning the justice of God's judgment on Rome. We were told earlier that the souls of the martyrs were underneath the altar in heaven. Their blood was spilt in the persecutions of Rome. Those martyrs, many of them slaves had borne the cups of water and wine to their Roman masters. Now it is only just that the very water supply of Rome be turned into blood. The ancient world knew the importance of a good water supply, for water was often hard to find and more difficult to transport. The Romans became the world's master aqueduct builders, transporting water miles from mountain sources to their large cities. The symbolism of Revelation becomes richly appropriate as the fresh water pouring into Rome becomes blood.

In the closing chapters of Revelation, John sees within the new Jerusalem "the river of the water of life, bright as crystal, flowing from the throne of God and of the Lamb" (22:1–2). Sermon themes might stress the contrast between this river of God providing salvation and life to the believers and the river of blood and destruction which characterized the last days of Rome. Rivers can become the source of life or death. Many countries of the world depend upon their rivers to be the very life source of their people. Yet, these same rivers in time of flood can become a threat to life and property. In Revelation, Rome's rivers and streams turned against her. In contrast in the closing scenes of Revelation, the saints stand by the River of Life and know the rewards of following the Lamb.

Plague on the Sun (16:8–9)

The Fourth Bowl is poured out upon the sun and its heat is intensified, scorching people with fire. In Trumpet Three, one-third of the heavenly bodies lost their light. The Fourth Bowl plague reminds us of the ninth Egyptian plague—the darkness which fell upon the land. John subdivides that plague into two manifestations—Bowls Four and Five. In contrast to the Egyptian plague the sun intensifies its heat in Bowl Four and immediately thereafter darkness settles over the kingdom of the beast (Bowl Five).

Again the punishment in Bowl Four is very appropriate for the sin. The Romans who have allowed their passions to burn so strongly are in turn scorched by the burning fire. John avers:

> "Come out of her, my people,
> lest you take part in her sins,
> lest you share in her plagues;
> for her sins are heaped high as heaven,
> and God has remembered her iniquities" (18:4–5).

Lactantius in his *Divine Institutes* (VII. 26) insists that in the last days God will cause the sun to stand still for three days, and its fire will punish the evil of the earth. In Revelation, the evil fires burning inside the hearts of the Romans are matched by the external fires of the sun.

Yet even after the first four bowls of wrath, "they cursed the name of God who had power over these plagues, and they did not repent and give him glory" (16:9). A sermon, "The Unrepentant Heart" might be used to explore some of the themes of Bowl Four. (1) Often when judgment is closest to us, we cannot perceive it. In the midst of World War II, Hitler's own officers plotted to assasinate him and came very close to doing it. Yet, Hitler did not perceive the act as a sign of the deep dissatisfaction in Germany against his leadership. He continued on the path that brought Germany to a fiery destruction. Even after the plagues of Egypt, Pharaoh did not relent in his persecution of the Hebrew people. In a similar vein, the Romans were blinded to their own iniquities and could not effect the changes needed in their lifestyle. (2) Evil is sometimes like a bed of quicksand, for once one falls into it, escape becomes very difficult. The more one struggles the more imprisoned he becomes. (3) True penance begins with the acceptance of God's mercy and restrained judgment.

Plague on the Beast's Throne (16:10–11)

The Fifth Bowl is poured out upon the kingdom of the beast and darkness overwhelms it. This bowl is directly related to the Fifth Trumpet, for John seems to view the monster locusts still at work. "Men gnawed their tongues in anguish and cursed the God of heaven for their pain ..." (16:10b–11). Earlier we said that the monster locusts represented the inner rot and decay of Rome. The very foundation of Roman society was in a state of decay and darkness was settling over the empire. Bowl Five brings that picture to fulfillment. Darkness has won, and the kingdom of Rome is shrouded in it.

Rot and decay bring with it pain and distress. People living in moral darkness have a high price to pay in terms of despair and lack of hope. However, sometimes people prefer the darkness instead of the light. Perhaps you have been mowing your grass on a hot summer day and turned over a rock by chance. Little creatures flee in every direction. They are accustomed to their world of darkness—light is an intruder. Surely, most of the Romans were used to the moral darkness upon the land. One can journey so far from the presence of God that one loses the desire to turn back. Perhaps you have had the experience as a visiting preacher for evangelistic services that the church wants you to visit all of the difficult people in the community to confront them with the Gospel. However, one soon realizes that some of these people enjoy their role of giving the visiting evangelist a difficult time. They have gotten to the point where they enjoy the darkness.

A sermon preached on this text might be entitled "The Finality of Darkness." One might begin with an illustration relating the story of the power failure in New York City a few summers ago. How strange it was to see the city of lights shrouded in darkness. People were trapped for hours in subways and elevators. There is something frightening about darkness. From there, one might deal first of all with the darkness of Rome. Relate the historical background of the Fifth Bowl in Revelation. The second point might stress the signs of moral darkness within our own land. The preacher could note here the ease with which one becomes accustomed to the realm of darkness. The third point of the sermon might be entitled "the light overwhelms the darkness." Christ is the light of the world—darkness cannot abide his presence. The sermon might conclude with the words: "The darkness is passing away and the true light is already shining" (I John 2:8).

Plague on the Euphrates (16:12–16)

The sixth angel pours his bowl upon the Euphrates river, and its water dries up to provide a way for the eastern kings to march against Rome. The Sixth Trumpet blast also took place at the Euphrates. At that time a crowd of two hundred million barbarians crossed the river to invade Rome. Some aspects of the Sixth Bowl also remind us of the second Egyptian plague in which multitudes of frogs swept across the land. In the Sixth Bowl, three frogs appear from the mouths of Satan and his two monster allies. These in turn go out to summon the whole world to assemble at the battlefield called Armageddon. In many world religions, the frog symbolizes evil or sinister forces. In the Iranian religion, frogs are presented as instruments of the evil god Ahriman. In many American Indian tribes, the frog also represents evil and can be seen inscribed on totem poles. In the apocalyptic symbolism of Revelation, the frog also stands for evil. Three frogs carry out the purposes of the dragon and his helpers. Their desire is to lead the world to worship Caesar and Roman power. They use any means available to them to trick and deceive the people on earth.

At this point, John interjects the voice of Christ, "Lo, I am coming like a thief! Blessed is he who is awake, keeping his garments that he may not go naked and be seen exposed!" (16:15). The mention of the great battle in verse fifteen reminds John that he also needs to insert a notice concerning the return of Christ. It is time for all true believers to be on guard, for the last days are at hand. Those who do not receive their immortal bodies will be naked and ashamed. Like ancient prisoners of war, they will be marched naked into captivity.

In 16:16, we find the only mention of the word Armageddon in Revelation and all of the NT. The battle does not actually take place at this time (not until 19:19), rather we hear only a summons to the battle. Armageddon as a proper name from the Hebrew refers to the mountain of Megiddo, a location in northern Israel in the southwestern fringe of the Esdraelon plain. Many ancient Israelite battles took place on that plain. Thus, John portrays the three frogs as bringing the kings of the earth to that location for one last struggle against the forces of the Lamb.

In Bowl Six the true face of evil appears—the face of a repulsive frog. So often in our world, evil is always painted with the most beautiful faces. Ugliness has never been a popular quality for the spirit of destructiveness in human society. A recent national publication listed as one of the seven major mortal sins as being over twenty-five. Evil never presents itself with the lined face of old age. Yet John dares to turn from the last plagues of God's judgment to the real picture of evil in the world. One might entitle a sermon on this passage as "The True Face of Evil." (1) If one could only present sin and evil in terms of the damage left in people's lives then perhaps the hideous faces of frogs would not be too far off the mark. (2) The true face of evil is destined to be seen for the forces of the Lamb will expose evil for what it is. (3) A final battle called Armageddon relates the symbolical truth that the way of righteousness will persevere.

Plague on the Air (16:17–21)

The final bowl is poured out upon Babylon or Rome. The punishment finally reaches the capital city. In Trumpet Seven the heavenly choir sang of God's final victory of evil. "The nations raged, but thy wrath came" (11:18). Bowl Seven brings this hymn into realization. In fact, we encounter a scene of completion and fulfillment. God's voice is heard from heaven uttering the dramatic words, "It is done" (16:17). The forces of nature erupt in one last destructive wave against the Roman empire. Hail stones, weighing a hundredweight pound the city. An earthquake splits the city into three parts. The grandeur of the destruction is so intense that "every island fled away, and no mountains were to be found" (16:20). John seemed to have been relying heavily here on Ezekiel's words of doom against God. "I will rain upon him and his hordes and the many peoples that are with him, torrential rains and hailstones, fire and brimstone" (Ezel. 38:22b).

"Babylon, the Great" is a good title for a sermon on the Seventh Vision of wrath. (1) The name Babylon brings to mind a people who have turned from God to selfish pursuits and endeavors. The ancient Jews might have thought of literal Babylon that city which led the Jews into captivity. The early Christians of A.D. 95 thought of the evil destructive forces of the Roman empire. (2) In a timeless sense, Babylon can symbolize the destructive forces of any power that opposes God. The image of many American cities has become one of despair and hopelessness. Unemployment, rape, murder, and poverty carve the face of our modern Babylons. (3) Yet over against the Babylons of the world stands the new Jerusalem, coming down from heaven. It is interesting that John's view of paradise is shaped in the form of a city. Babylon and the new Jerusalem stand side by side. Babylon is doomed to judgment whereas Jerusalem represents our hopes and aspirations.

Visions of Babylon's Fall
(Revelation 17:1—20:3)

The dire results of the bowl plagues are spelled out in extensive detail in Rev 17:1–20:3. John views the fall of Rome as the beginning point for the last stages of human history. In fact more pages of Revelation are devoted to the fall of Rome than any other subject. The battle of Armageddon is described in three verses as well as the millennial reign. However, John takes almost three whole chapters to depict the destruction of the enemy power—Rome. It is a section filled with many laments and hymns. Perhaps this part of Revelation more than any other had existential meaning for John's first century readers. Because many of them had lost loved ones in the persecutions of Caesar Domitian, it would have been only natural to have yearned for a day of retribution for the Roman empire. John is therefore very careful to give every detail of the judgment of wicked Babylon or Rome.

It is very interesting that no aspect of the heavenly temple is highlighted in this judgment section. In the Visions of Wrath, we were told that the Holy of Holies was filled with smoke and that one could no longer view the Ark of the Covenant. Now the temple building looms in the background but all eyes are fixed upon the burning city of Rome. The time of opportunity and acceptance of God's mercy has passed. The bowl plagues had only caused the Romans to curse the name of God rather than to repent.

The thing that most impresses the reader concerning John's portrayal of God in Revelation is the emphasis which has been placed on his patience and mercy in dealing with human beings. Unlike the portrayal of so many current popular books on Revelation, John's picture is not full of an angry God throwing thunderbolts down from heaven. Sermons on God's judgment should always emphasize God is not "out to get" human beings. In the Bible, one confronts the opposing picture that God is never willing to give upon human kind. He holds on even when we turn our backs and journey into darkness. Even the plagues, as gruesome as they are, are designed to bring about repentance. The Romans chose their own way and had to live with the results of their decision.

In a sermon called, "Freedom of Choice," the preacher might emphasize the following truths: (1) The choices which we make in life have their own long-lasting results. Even the choice of a vocation made at an early age determines the type of lifestyle that one might expect down through life. (2) The choice to follow the way of the cross brings with it a lifestyle of commitment and service. A choice to live life apart from Christ brings with it certain options as well. The wonderful thing about it all is that God does allow us to make the choice. Yet at the same time, his creatures must hear the consequences of that choice. (3) The history of man is also a story of God attempting to reach out to his creation—even by risking to come in the form of human flesh in Jesus Christ. Thus, the judgment scenes in the final chapters of Revelation are truly sad because of the lost opportunities represented. These are themes that cry out for proclamation.

Babylon as a Harlot (17:1-18)

The scenes in this section of Revelation directly manifest the end results of the Visions of Wrath. "Then one of the seven angels who had the seven bowls came and said to me, 'Come, I will show you the judgment of the great harlot who is seated upon many waters'" (17:1). We see immediately that John uses one of the seven angels of the bowl plagues to point out the results of those plagues. The first judgment is directly upon Babylon or Rome; the great capital city is depicted as a harlot rather than as a goddess. Throughout Revelation Babylon is a code name for Rome. We here encounter John's use of symbolism at its very best. A monster beast appears on the scene, and its rider is a woman bedecked as a harlot. The beast itself is obviously the Roman empire. John even leaves us a clue behind at this point, "The seven heads are seven hills on which the woman is seated" (17:9). No one needs to think twice about the identity of this beast since the seven hills of Rome were just as famous then as they are now. This beast is quite likely the same one as depicted coming up out of the sea in chapter thirteen, for both beasts are said to have seven heads and ten horns. In chapter thirteen, the symbolism had to do more with the seven Caesars than the seven hills. However, John also feels free to shift around his symbolism and also use the Caesars in chapter seventeen as well.

The woman on the beast is gaudily dressed, arrayed in purple and scarlet, gold and jewels and pearls. What better symbolism could be found for the ostentatious capital city? Even Roman writers of the first century characterized the capital city as the real heart of the empire. The worship of Rome and Domitian held the far flung empire together. However, John can see the true nature of Rome—she is nothing other than a harlot. She has shared her immorality with the whole world. In the vision, the woman has a brand on her forehead, "Babylon the great, mother of harlots and of earth's abominations" (17:5). In ancient Rome, many of the harlots had shaved heads and the brand "P" (standing for *Porne* or prostitute) on their foreheads. The woman of John's vision holds a cup full of abominations, and the blood of the martyrs. The abominations might well refer to the blasphemies of the Caesar cults. The woman has become drunk from the blood of the saints and the martyrs (17:6). In a very clever way, John is able to capture all of the evil of Rome in the image of a Roman harlot drunk on the blood of God's people. One senses that Rome is ripe for judgment—God's people have suffered far too long.

John goes on to present the identity of the seven heads of the beast in riddle form:

> "They are also seven kings, five of whom have fallen, one is, the other has not yet come, and when he comes he must remain only a little white. As for the beast that was and is not, it is an eighth but it belongs to the seven, and it goes to perdition" (17:10–11).

Many attempts have been made to solve this riddle. The best solution seems to be to view the five fallen Casesars as Tiberius, Caligula, Claudius, Vespasian, and Titus. This approach involves starting the list with Caesar Tiberius who was ruling at the time of the crucifixion of Christ. It also means leaving out Galba, Otho, and Vitellius, who altogether reigned less than two years. Many Romans viewed them as renegades rather than kings. The term "one is" refers to Domitian. The one "who is yet to come" refers to Nero whom many Romans believed had never died and would return to rule over the Roman empire. In the discussion of chapter thirteen of Revelation, we pointed out the widespread Nero redivivus myth. Nero is viewed as an eighth king even though he belonged to the seven. In reality, John is basically concerned here with this eighth king—Nero. He would come from hiding among the Parthians east of the Euphrates and lead the ten Parthian armies against Rome.

The return of Nero is depicted in 17:16-17 in the symbolism of the seven headed beast turning on the harlot and leaving her for dead in the city's streets. "They will make her desolate and naked, and devour her flesh and burn her up with fire" (17:16). Ezekiel had foretold a similar prophecy against Jerusalem, "They shall also strip you of your clothes and take away your fine jewels" (Ezek 23:26). Although the beast and the ten kings have success against Rome, they will utterly fail against the Lamb and his followers. "They will make war on the Lamb, and the Lamb will conquer them" (17:14).

The First Judgment is aimed directly at the Roman empire. John's symbol of a harlot truly represents the depraved spirit of the ancient city. In preaching on chapter seventeen, one might well compare the harlot of chapter seventeen with mother Israel of chapter twelve. The harlot sits on the beast whereas mother Israel stands on the sun. Mother Israel brings forth a baby, the Messiah, while the harlot produces death and destruction. Mother Israel flees to the desert for safe keeping while the harlot makes her dwelling place in the desert to bring havoc and evil to the earth. In the female image of chapter twelve, one finds the message of hope for the world. In the image of the harlot, one confronts the face of sin and decay of human society. The Romans worshiped a two-headed God by the name of Janus: one head looked forward and one backward. We call the first month of our calendar January in honor of that god, for January is a time for looking forward and backward in our lives. The harlot and mother Israel represent two ways of viewing life in the first century world and the present. The harlot calls to mind the idol worship, immorality, and the abuse of human society. Mother Israel causes us to look forward to the rule of God in his kingdom. It is the face of hope as reflected in the countenance of a new born baby. She points to a time of peace on earth, goodwill to men.

Babylon's Doom Foretold (18:1-24)

The Second Vision brings a close-up view of the fall of Babylon or Rome. In modern times, it would be like a newsreel team showing us the ravished streets and disrupted lifestyle of a bombed-out city. John is at his very best in describing a major city—Rome—that has fallen. The scene is punctuated by funeral laments or dirges in the background. One gets the feeling that a gigantic movie screen is needed to capture the force of what John is portraying.

In fact, a stage would be best suited to present the sheer drama of these scenes. In the background Rome would be in flames and various actors cross the front part of the stage to present messages of doom to Babylon. The first such voice comes from an angel possessing great authority. He announces in a mighty voice, "Fallen, fallen is Babylon the great!" Christians hearing those words in the first century churches would have jumped with joy. Babylon or Rome was their oppressor, and thus was now getting exactly what it deserved. The angel goes on to tell us why Rome has fallen. The primary reason seems to be that she has shared her immorality with the whole earth. "For all nations have drunk the wine of her impure passion" (18:3).

A second voice, unidentified, declares another message (18:4-8), which sets forth the justice of what has happened to Rome. The call is for God to "repay her double for her deeds" (18:6). The sins of Rome are so great that they are literally "heaped high as heaven." The message also includes the announcement for the believers to leave the city so that they will not be involved in her punishment. Over against this voice of judgment one hears the voice of Rome, "A queen I sit, I am no widow, mourning I shall never see" (18:7). This insolent voice of Rome makes the described judgments as being all the more deserved. For the early Christians those words of boasting had been heard more than once. How hard it must have been for them to conceive of Rome in ashes and consumed with fire. In periods of persecution, the righteous seem to be on the losing team. However, this section of Revelation underscores God's ultimate victory. Even the power of

Rome could not prevail before God's judgment. Christians need to hear preached more often the victorious note of the faith.

The angelic announcements are followed by three funeral dirges chanted by the kings, merchants, and shipmasters. We shall look at each of these in turn.

(1) As the capital city of the ancient world, Rome attracted vassal kings from many empires. Revelation has emphasized many times that Rome shared her immorality with the world. The kings of the empire stand a long way off and mourn the fall of the city. Rome is burning in the background and the kings are chanting their funeral dirge in the foreground. The funeral dirge itself is very close to Ezekiel's laments over Tyre (Ezek 26:16–17; 27:35). The whole scene is also very similar to that of Euripides' Greek tragic drama, *The Trojan Women*, in which three different groups come on stage to mourn burning Troy. The lament of the kings watching burning Rome echoes across the stage:

"Alas! alas! thou great city,
thou mighty city, Babylon!
In one hour has thy judgment come!" (18:10).

The Greek word for alas is *ouai*, the same word John used for the screech of an eagle in the Seven Trumpets section. The cry of the eagle of doom and destruction has come true. These kings though weeping over the city are careful not to get too close. They do not want to participate in her judgment. It is so true of life that when times are good and prosperous friendships are easy to make. Yet, when bad luck and misfortune fall, some fairweather friends disappear. Even Job's friends who remained with him during his bad times counseled him to seek death.

(2) The second funeral dirge is chanted by the merchants who once traded their wares in Rome. Their major concern is that "no one buys their cargo any more" (18:11). Rome was the great center of commerce of the ancient world; from North Africa gold, ivory, and costly wood products, from India jewels and pearls, spices from Arabia, cinnamon from South China, myrrh from Medea, purple and silk from Asia Minor, wheat from Egypt, horses from Armenia, chariots from Gaul, slaves from Israel and the rest of the world. The

market places of Rome were crowded with merchandise from all over the world. These prosperous merchants stand afar and chant their dirge:

> "The fruit for which thy soul longed has gone from thee, and all thy dainties and thy splendor are lost to thee, never to be found again!" (18:14).

This sad note is continued in the second stanza of the dirge:

> "Alas, alas, for the great city
> that was clothed in fine linen, in purple and scarlet,
> bedecked with gold, with jewels, and with pearls!
> In one hour all this wealth has been laid waste" (18:16–17a).

Again destruction had come upon Rome very quickly—even in the midst of buying and selling. One is almost reminded of the ancient city of Pompei in the terrible earthquake of A.D. 79. Today walking through the ruins one views the city in the midst of everyday activity unaware of its coming doom. Food is on the tables and merchants at their work. That activity was frozen into the very lava that covered the city.

(3) The third funeral dirge is sung by the shipmasters and sailors who frequented the port of Rome. The great sea power of Rome was known around the Mediterranean world. Into its ports came ships bearing the riches of the empire. It is only fitting then that the shipmasters and sailors bewail the fall of Rome. They, too, stand a long way off and chant their funeral dirge:

> "Alas, alas, for the great city
> where all who had ships at sea grew rich by her wealth!
> In one hour she has been laid waste" (18:19).

The grandeur of Rome proved to be as fleeting as many of the other great world empires that have risen only to fall. One need only to remember the colossal plans of Hitler in building the German Reich. The best architects in Germany were hired to plan and design a new city of Berlin which would reflect the pride and glory of the Nazi regime. Then one should contrast the pictures of Berlin in ruins following the bombing raids of World War II. In a similar vein, John wants us to see the splendors of Rome contrasted with its mighty fall. Every dramatic tool available to him is used in chapter eighteen of Revelation. One might see many values for preaching in this section of laments and funeral dirges. In a sermon, "The Brevity of Life," we might ponder the transient nature of so many things that we value and adore. (1) Human beings work and labor to gain the materialistic things of the world that will only decay and become the sought out archeological treasure of the next generation. (2) The Lamb stands above the ruins of Rome symbolizing the true life and values that endure. The Caesars thought that they had given Christianity a death blow, but history proved the enduring quality of the Christian faith and the transient nature of Rome's power and glory. (3) Believers must choose between the things that are brief and transient and those that will endure into the Kingdom of God.

Following the funeral laments, a voice in heaven calls out for rejoicing in heaven. Those who have opposed God's people and tortured the martyrs have fallen. To punctuate that statement, a mighty angel throws a large stone like a millstone upon the sea which destroys the last vestiges of the empire. John indicates the totality of the destruction by pointing out some of the aspects of life missing in the city.

> "The sound of harpers and minstrels, of flute players and trumpeters,
> shall be heard in thee no more" (18:22).

A city in destruction has no more need for festive music. The sound of craftsmen and millers are no longer heard in the city streets. Such basic evidence of life in a city as light is missing. The festive voices of wedding parties also are no longer heard.

The reason for this vast destruction of Rome which has just been depicted is expressed quite simply by John:

> "And in her was found the blood of prophets and of saints,
> and of all who have been slain on earth" (18:24).

The saints have persevered to the end and have won the victory. What Roman of the first century could have possibly imagined a small group of slaves and ex-slaves as winning out in the struggle with the empire? However, that is exactly what happened. God's justice had been manifested to the whole Roman world.

Babylon's Fall Celebrated in Heaven (19:1–10)

The laments on earth concerning the fall of Babylon are answered in heaven with hymns of rejoicing and thanksgiving. The first hymn (19:1b–3) is sung by a great multitude in heaven. The focus of the hymn is upon the justice of God in bringing his judgment upon Babylon or Rome. The cry of "Hallelujah" echoes across the courts of heaven. As a consequence of viewing God's judgment, the heavenly court is called to worship, "Salvation and glory and power belong to our God" (19:1). Great emphasis is placed upon the fact that he has judged "the great harlot" (19:2). The heavenly hosts are just as happy as the earthly saints that God, "has avenged on her [Rome] the blood of his servants" (19:2b). The smoke of Rome's burning will rise forever and ever.

Such glee and joy in heaven over the fall of Rome might be misunderstood among Christians of the modern world. Is it truly Christian to celebrate the fall of an enemy? However, it is easy to ask that question nearly two thousand years after Rome's oppression of the Christians. As we have said earlier, the first-century Christians who had lost loved ones in the Roman persecutions might well have felt joy in hearing of Rome's judgment and destruction. In a timeless sense, the hymn seems to reflect a message of the ultimate destruction of evil in the world. Rome symbolizes the enemy of God in every age. The preacher must stress here the theme of God's final victory of evil. It is good to know that the Caesars, Hitlers, Stalins, and Idi Amins of this world will not be the ultimate controlling forces of our planet.

With the ultimate destruction of evil, a heavenly choir made up of multitudes sings concerning the marriage feast of the Lamb (19:6–9). Throughout the OT, the relation of God to Israel is often expressed in terms of marriage. The same symbol is taken over by the NT to speak of Christ's relation to the church. Many of the Old Testament prophets viewed Israel as a faithless wife to Yahweh. However, they expected that one day God would renew the marriage relationship with Israel. Hosea expressed that hope, "And in that day, says the LORD, you will call me, 'My husband' . . ." (2:16). According to Ephesians 5:25–27, the church is at present the bride of Christ, but there is also a future expectation of the consummation of that promise: "that he might present the church to himself in splendor, without spot or wrinkle" (Ephes 5:27). The final marriage festival will take place with the appearance of the Lamb. Many Jews expected a feast or celebration around a messianic banquet table with the invited guests reclining on couches with Abraham and the Messiah. Isaiah shared that expectation, "On this mountain the LORD of hosts will make for all peoples a feast of fat things, a feast of wine on the lees" (Isa 25:6).

John views the Bride as ready for the marriage because she has clothed herself in righteous deeds. Great emphasis has been placed on works and deeds all the way through Revelation. These works stand as the ultimate testimony to the faith in the hearts of believers. With the fall of Babylon or Rome and the faithful testimony of the churches, everything now is ready for the marriage supper of the Lamb. It is not surprising that one of the seven beatitudes in Revelation reads, "Blessed are those who are invited to the marriage supper of the Lamb" (19:9).

The positive stress placed on celebration and rejoicing outweighs any undue preoccupation with the destruction and judgment themes in Revelation. The preacher must try hard to help his congregation free themselves from being frightened by Revelation. This passage is a good place to stress the joy of fulfillment of the promises of God for his faithful. It is interesting that the sound of wedding music drowns out the notes of funeral dirges in the final chapters of John's work. Revelation says much to us of what it means to rejoice in the Lord. John never portrays heaven as a somber place but one of constant music, singing and shouting. There is an important message in the fact that the return of Christ is described as a great wedding feast. Every Jew realized that a marriage feast meant joy and feasting—the most elaborate of all festivals. How exciting to view one's faith in those kind of terms.

In a sermon entitled, "Joy, Joy, Joy," the basic themes of joy in the Kingdom might be explored: (1) the joy of the invitation to the Kingdom (19:9), (2) the joy of the messianic banquet (19:7), and (3) the joy of readiness for the Kingdom (19:8).

Babylon's Conqueror (19:11-16)

The Fourth Vision brings about the return of the Messiah—here portrayed as a warrior king who will destroy wicked Babylon and the nations which had opposed the people of God. Some Jews expected this type of warrior Messiah. Isaiah declared,

> "I have trodden the wine press alone,
>   and from the peoples no one was with me;
> I trod them in my anger
>   and trampled them in my wrath;
> their lifeblood is sprinkled upon my garments,
>   and I have stained all my raiment" (Isa 63:3).

The Jews expected the Messiah to overwhelm their enemies and give them the victory. Thus John describes the Messiah, here, as dressed in a robe that had been dipped in blood. He leads a great army of heavenly hosts. "From his mouth issues a sharp sword with which to smite the nations, and he will rule them with a rod of iron" (19:15). What nation or army could resist this kind of power? Nero leading the Parthian kings could have no possible hope of success. The final battle of Armageddon is now at hand.

Even in the midst of all the rhetoric of generals and warfare, the title which the Messiah bears is "The Word of God" (19:13). Many scholars have noted this as a favorite title for Jesus in the Johannine writings. Even though few would see John as the author for all the Johannine writings, the title may have been used for Jesus in a Johannine school. It is evident that John has painted his portrait of the return of Christ in highly symbolic language. The interpreter is not to think of literal heavenly armies and a warrior Messiah. The military language points rather to the power of the Word of God. No one is able to resist it for the Lamb is the living Word of God. The symbol of the Lamb with seven horns and eyes now disappears in Revelation to be replaced with the Word of God on a white horse of victory. The name written on his thigh says it all, "King of kings and Lord of lords" (19:16).

The preacher needs to expand on the title Word of God. So many believers have a very limited view of God's word. For some the "word" is the written record or Bible. In fact, the Bible becomes an object of worship and some believers might be accused of idol worship. In contrast, at the heart of the Christian faith is the living word of God—Jesus Christ. That word becomes the point of judging all other revelation from God. A similar view is found in Wisdom 18:15, "Thine all powerful word leaped from heaven out of the royal throne, a stern warrior, into the midst of the doomed land, bearing a shared sword thine unfeigned commandment." One might entitle a sermon preached on this passage, "The Living Word of God." The points which should be developed are: (1) the origin of the Word (19:11), (2) the piercing nature of the Word (19:15), and (3) the victory of the Word (19:16).

Babylon's Demise Announced (19:17-18)

In the Fifth Vision an angel announces the battle which will bring the demise of Babylon. The birds of prey are summoned to the battlefield "to eat the flesh of kings, the flesh of captains, the flesh of mighty men, the flesh of horses and their riders, and the flesh of all men" (19:18). Throughout Revelation, the reader senses the tension building toward one last struggle between good and evil. In chapter twelve, John laid the foundation for such a battle in presenting the struggle between Satan and his allies and the new-born Messiah. When Satan failed to destroy the Messiah, he turned his attention to the woman and her descendants, the Christian Church. The final victory of the righteous is so secure that the angel standing on the sun can announce it even before it begins. The imagery for this passage has been borrowed by John from Ezek 39:17. There the birds of prey are called to gather to feast on the dead on the battlefields of Gog.

In essence, John has reversed the wedding supper of the Lamb which has just been announced for the righteous (19:6-9). The birds of prey are the invited guests to dine upon the bodies of the anti-Christ and his followers. John adds to the list of the doomed men in Ezekiel, the names of "all men, both free and slave, both small and great" (19:18). All of mankind that follows the leadership of the anti-Christ will taste defeat in the coming battle. No hope is offered to anyone who follows the evil forces into conflict. They will quickly meet their doom. Before the battle they may have feasted on birds and animals, but after the battle, they will become the food for these same animals.

The message of the angel on the sun is in reality a nightmare—almost too hideous to comprehend. How many armies would march off to war if they were shown films of the aftermath of the battle beforehand? Yet, as we have seen so often in Revelation, the warning issued to the evil of the world has been largely ignored or overlooked. God's mercy is without limit, yet the time finally comes when righteousness must prevail and evil be vanquished. Human beings can ignore warning signs of ill health in their own physical bodies until it is too late for physicians to affect a cure. There is a sad note in Revelation's depiction of the gory feast of the birds. Such destruction could have been avoided if the evil forces had heeded the signs of God's rule about them.

A sermon could be developed around 19:17-18 emphasizing the "Dangers of Procrastination." Stress should be placed upon the fact that individuals know what action should be taken but often avoid making the important decisions which would implement it. One might emphasize in the first part of the sermon the lessons drawn from the history of Israel. Over and over again Israel resisted the messages of Hosea and Amos. Finally destruction came upon them brought about by the Assyrian army. The Southern Jews procrastinated in regard to the appeals of Jeremiah and Isaiah until the forces of Babylon swept down upon them.

The second part of the sermon might deal with the slowness of the Jews of the first century world to respond to the teaching of Jesus. We all remember that poignant scene with Jesus on the Mount of Olives looking out over the city of Jerusalem weeping at the rejection of his people. Then the last part of the sermon might concern itself with the final scenes of history as depicted in Revelation. Man does not learn the lessons of history but procrastinates in responding to the initiatives of God until it is too late.

Babylon's Final Battle (19:19-21)

The sixth scene in this section views the judgment of God in terms of the actual battle of Armageddon—Babylon's last conflict. Although John only mentions the battle by its proper name in one place (16:16), it is obvious that the same battle is being described here. With the parousia of Christ, the end time events take place very rapidly. There has been

Revelation 17:1—20:3

much debate among scholars concerning the actual location of Armageddon. The word *Ar* comes from the Hebrew word for hill (*Har*). *Mageddon* is the Hebrew term for Megiddo, a famous biblical city located on the southern fringe of the plain of Esdraelon in Galilee. Thus the place name probably refers to the mountains of Megiddo. We know that the final battle in Ezekiel (38:8) is depicted at the "mountains of Israel." Daniel also speaks of the death of Antiochus somewhere between the sea and the glorious holy mountain (Dan 11:45). Some scholars have suggested that the place name has become somewhat distorted in Revelation. Originally it was *har migdon* or "fruitful mountain." Thus the mountain singled out might be Jerusalem as the "navel of the earth" or some other mountain in Israel (Joel 3:1; Zech 14:2–3).

In favor of Megiddo on the Esdraelon plain would be the numerous battles of Israel throughout her history fought near there. This plain is roughly triangular in shape and serves to separate Galilee from Samaria. It begins in the west near modern Haifa and runs eastward almost to the Sea of Galilee. A famous road in the ancient world leading from Egypt to Syria passed along the coast of Palestine, cut inland near modern Haifa, and then ran across the Esdraelon plain to Syria. The city of Megiddo was one of the oldest cities along that route. Numerous levels of civilizations have been found by archeologists on the site. The whole nearby area played a very important role in the history of the Israelites. By the "waters of Megiddo" (Judg 5:19–21), Deborah defeated the great armies of Sisera and Pharaoh Neco overwhelmed Josiah and his forces (II Kings 23:29–30). The city of Megiddo became a valuable fortress city for Solomon, Hezekiah and other Jewish kings. The plain itself would see many famous battles during the Maccabean period and Roman times. Later Napoleon would fight there and the English would defeat the Turks there in 1917. In every way of looking at it, the plain of Megiddo (Esdraelon) was the classical battlefield of Israel. Zechariah expressed the feelings of so many Jews concerning Megiddo when he declared, "On that day the mourning in Jerusalem will be as great as the mourning for Hadadrimmon in the plain of Megiddo" (12:11). The very place name evoked feelings of sadness and doom.

From this background, it seems self-evident that John has brought together two basic ideas "the glorious mountain" where the enemy armies gather and the classic battlefield tradition from Megiddo. Hence we have before us not so much a literal battle on some specific battlefield but rather a symbolic spiritual struggle between good and evil. It is amazing the ends to which many popular interpreters of Revelation will go in terms of describing actual battles with machine guns and tanks. These bible teachers have all the battle plans outlined and know exactly which nations are going to participate in the battle. They follow the latest news from the Middle East even more closely than the local news media. They have it all worked out with elaborate charts and graphs which have everything pinpointed in precise detail. Revelation, in contrast, does not purport to give us the detailed design of the battle of Armageddon. In fact, it seems that once Christ appears on earth, what fighting has been going on quickly stops. The army of heaven does not even lift one sword. The living Word of God overwhelms the forces of Babylon and the anti-Christ by his very appearance. "And the rest were slain by the sword of him who sits upon the horse, the sword that issues from his mouth" (19:21). In fact, John takes only three verses to describe the whole battle.

The two beasts, allies of Satan, are captured and thrown alive into the lake of fire. Their time of deception is now over. Satan in contrast is placed into prison for a thousand years. The great victory depicted in this passage should bring great assurance to believers down through the ages. The Word of God is far mightier than any human word. In the world of the first century, Caesar's word carried great weight. However, we have seen that the power of Rome or Babylon could not resist the living Word of God. Even Satan's word as manifested in the two beasts pales in significance to the Word of God. There is no real dualistic picture in Revelation as one finds in so many other apocalyptic works. The word of Satan is never placed on a par with that of the living Word. Even in the description of the battle of Armageddon Satan never directly opposes Christ. The power of Satan is so limited that an angel rather than Christ carries out the work of binding him. A sermon dealing with the "Limitations of Evil" might reassure many church members who live in fear of Satan and the world of evil. One might point out the places in Revelation where evil does not prevail. For example, Satan fails to destroy the infant in chapter twelve and also lacks the power to overcome Michael and the angels in heaven. He also has missed the opportunity to overwhelm the woman and her descendants—the Christian Church. The greatest failure of all is in the final battle against the Word of God. One, of course, must never take evil for granted and ignore its ability to bring destruction into life. Yet, the Christian is convinced that evil shall never control the ultimate destiny of the world, for at the cross Satan was decisively defeated by Christ.

Babylon's Leader Enchained (20:1-3)

The Seventh Vision comes upon Babylon's leader—Satan himself. An angel captures him and locks him up for a thousand years. Many world religions (Persian, Egyptian, Mandaean, Scandinavian, and Germanic) have a similar story concerning the defeat of evil forces. Isaiah declared:

> On that day the Lord will punish
> the host of heaven, in heaven,
> and the kings of the earth, on the earth.
> They will be gathered together
> as prisoners in a pit;
> they will be shut up in a prison,
> and after many days they will be punished (24:21-22).

A similar injunction is found in the Prayer of Manasseh:

> who hast confined the ocean by the word of command
> who has shut up the abyss and sealed it with thy fearful and glorious name (v. 3, neb).

However, unlike the stories in other religions, John speaks of the release of Satan at the end of thousand years. Satan's ultimate defeat will not come until his days of imprisonment are over. Then there will be one last struggle between good and evil called the battle of Gog and Magog. The Israelite tradition stressed a complete reign of the Messiah on earth with all of his power and glory. As long as evil is in existence, the full glory of this Messianic reign cannot be manifested. The idea of an intermediate Messianic reign seems to have evolved in Judaism at a time when the Israelites had not quite given up on a literal reign of the Messiah in Jerusalem. However, more and more they were looking forward to a new transcendental age in which all the messianic promises would be realized. The intermediate reign—in Revelation a thousand years—is designed as a time of vindication for the Lamb and the Christian martyrs.

Paradise is paradise because all evil is missing and no longer has any force. It is difficult for human beings living in a world where evil is so prevalent to imagine a time when it will be imprisoned. Yet every believer yearns for the day when righteousness will be manifested and the justice of God will be vindicated. At times even now we can see signs of a world that God must have originally intended—a world where evil and destruction is not present. Even in a world where evil is present, glimpses of beauty occasionally shine through. Perhaps a sermon on this passage could contrast the irony of Satan in chains with the chains humans receive in following the way of evil. The one who has imprisoned so many, finally ends up in chains himself. A sermon on this topic could be entitled, "The End of Evil." Three points could be developed: (1) evil's brief rule (19:19), (2) evil's struggle with good (19:20), and (3) evil is chained (20:2).

Visions of Fulfillment
(Revelation 20:4—22:5)

The theme of promise and fulfillment runs throughout the last section of Revelation. The time has come to reveal to the faithful Christians what God has prepared for them. In describing the new age, John continues to make rich use of symbolism. Apocalyptic literature places great emphasis on the theme of two ages: an old one which is passing away and a new one which is dawning. Of course the apocalyptic writer is much more interested in the new age rather than the old. He likes to give elaborate discriptions of every aspect of this dawning age. Thus, it should be no surprise that John places such great stress on describing the beauty and joy of the new age.

John's view of the new age can almost be expressed in terms of "paradise regained." His description of the dawning era reminds us very much of the Garden of Eden stories in Genesis. God walked with his created beings and his presence was felt everywhere. There was no separation between God and the created order. In Revelation, a similar kind of picture is painted—heaven and earth are no longer separated. God and the Lamb dwell in the midst of the saints. One new aspect of the discription over against Genesis is the emphasis placed upon the holy city Jerusalem. The focus of the new order is a city rather than the garden. The fruit trees and river, typical paradise discriptions are there, but John puts more stress on measuring city walls, pinpointing the material of the streets and gates.

One might find preaching on John's view of paradise more relevant to today's world than the view set forth in Genesis. A good number of modern Christians live in cities and are acquainted with city life. A sermon using a text based on the Visions of Fulfillment might contrast the city of Revelation with our own modern cities. In our modern cities, we know well the meaning of robbery, pain, poverty, and lack of hope. In John's description of the heavenly city, we are told of a community devoid of sickness, pain, and death. There is no robbery or other crimes because people of such inclination are without the city in the lake of fire. The preacher must be careful to avoid the great emphasis placed upon the materialistic aspect of the city: pearly gates, golden streets and bejeweled foundations. That theme has been so overworked in churches that one often encounters a crass materialism in such interpretations. The community theme with God at its center is a much better approach.

Fulfillment of the Millennium (20:4-10)

The First Vision features a thousand year reign for Christ and the martyrs. Perhaps no other subject in Revelation has become so debated in recent times. Theories abound concerning the subject, and schools of disciples have formed around the various points of view: premillennial, postmillennial, or amillennial. Some churches place on their outdoor bulletin boards the name of the school to which they adhere. Many pastors avoid preaching on Revelation for fear of causing dissent or disruption in their congregations. Perhaps no other subject in the book has caused such a barrier to be erected against studying Revelation.

The problem with the various millennial schools is that they all involve rules and regulations for interpreting the whole book of Revelation. Thus it is almost deceiving to refer to them as millennial schools for they are all concerned with more than the millennium as set forth in Rev 20:4-6. In fact in some of these schools, one must buy a scheme for interpreting the whole Bible. After reading the volumes of material written on all three schools, it comes as a shock to most people to discover that Revelation devotes only three verses to the subject. Even more astonishing, one soon ascertains, that the millennium is mentioned nowhere else in the NT. One of the most important tasks in preaching on the millennium is to establish that it is not one of the central themes of the NT. A case must be made to let Revelation stand on its own—allow its narrative be heard apart from any schemes concerning the millennium. The pastor might do an introductory sermon in which a few words would be said about each of the basic views, and then do a role play of a leading personality in each school. In such a sermon, the particular view in question should be made as simple as possible. The basic subject of the millennium should be the point of contact. Hence, the premillennial school emphasizes the return of Christ to the earth before the millennium and his decisive rule during the subsequent one thousand years. The postmillennial school places stress upon the millennium as the rule of the church on earth while Christ is still in heaven. The amillennial school interprets the millennium in a symbolical sense—Christ started to rule at his resurrection and will continue to do so for a complete period of time. Following that introduction, one could deal with the three basic verses in Revelation on the subject. It would be well to read the verses aloud so that the congregation would be impressed with the brevity of the passage.

The idea of an interim or temporary messianic reign between the ages has its roots in Jewish apocalyptic literature. In II Esdras 5:2—7:4, a messianic interim reign of four hundred years is described. During that time the Messiah and those who have gone to heaven without dying rule over the earth. At the end of that period these rulers will die and then be resurrected to start a new age. A similar pattern is found in II Enoch 32:3—33:1 but without a messianic figure. World history is presented as consisting of seven days—each a thousand years in duration. The seventh thousand year period is one of rest before the dawn of an eighth which will be the new age. Some Jewish apocalypses have no interim reign at all (Apocalypses of Abraham, Daniel, and the Assumption of Moses).

John may have drawn other ideas of a messianic reign from the Book of Ezekiel (chaps. 36—39). The basic outline of the last few chapters of Revelation seems to fit within the scope of Ezekiel:

> "Behold, I will take the people of Israel from the nations among which they have gone, and will gather them from all sides, and bring them to their own land" (37:21).
>
> "My servant David shall be king over them; and they shall all have one shepherd" (37:24).

Here in Ezekiel a strong emphasis is placed on a kingdom of God's people ruled again by David. Ezekiel also mentions a revolt by Gog of the land of Magog. Revelation has such a battle at the end of the one thousand year messianic reign.

Following the battle against God, Ezekiel speaks of a new Jerusalem which would be the home of the blessed: "And brought me in the visions of God into the land of Israel, and set me down upon a very high mountain, on which was a structure like a city opposite me" (40:2).

At this point, one might want to preach a sermon comparing Ezekiel's and John's views of the messianic age. The preacher might underline the concept of God's visible rule among his people. There seems to be a hope in both testaments for a renewal of the earth. Paul stated this hope well, "creation itself will be set free from its bondage to decay" (Rom 8:21). In one sense that hope is now being fulfilled in Christ but yet there is also a point of culmination for that expectation. We surely can speak of Christ reigning in our world and that in one sense Satan has been defeated at the cross. Yet there seems to be in John's mind a longing for some visual rule of Christ in the world in terms of a messianic kingdom. These thoughts might be expressed in a sermon "The Rule of Christ": (1) the beginning of the rule—the cross, (2) the power of the rule—The Holy Spirit, and (3) the fulfillment of the rule—the parousia.

Let us now look more closely at the three verses in Revelation devoted to the millennium.

> Then I saw thrones, and seated on them were those to whom judgment was committed. Also I saw the souls of those who had been beheaded for their testimony to Jesus and for the word of God, and who had not worshiped the beast or its image and had not received its mark on their foreheads or their hands. They came to life, and reigned with Christ a thousand years. The rest of the dead did not come to life again until the thousand years were ended. This is the first resurrection. Blessed and holy is he who shares in the first resurrection! Over such the second death has no power, but they shall be priests of God and of Christ, and they shall reign with him a thousand years (20:4-6).

If one reads the verses carefully on their own merit rather than from the point of some millennial school, one soon sees the special role given to the martyrs. Those who rule with Christ are "those who have been beheaded," or the martyrs. All the way through Revelation the work and role of the Christian martyrs have been highlighted. The preacher must be appreciative of their role in the millennium. In the messianic reign there will be a great opportunity for all to see the vindication of the martyrs. In chapter six, God told the martyrs under the heavenly altar to rest until their number was complete. The world would be judged and their blood vindicated. This is why a millennium is a great necessity in Revelation. The martyrs are given their thrones, and they rule with Christ for the thousand years. To make the identity of the group even more certain, John goes on to declare that the ones on the thrones have been beheaded for their testimony to Christ and that they have not borne the mark of the beast. In 13:15, John told us that those who will not worship the image of the beast are slain. The group ruling on the thrones in the millennium, have been slain and must "come to life again" to exercise their rule.

In 20:5–6, the "rest" of the dead are resurrected. The righteous will inherit eternal life with the martyrs in the new Jerusalem. The unrighteous dead will be placed in the lake of fire with the two beasts and Satan. A sermon on the glorious rule of the martyrs could be called the "Dawn of Hope." One might contrast the martyrs' earthly lives with their exalted rule in the millennium. These Christians were at the bottom rung of the world's society. They lived in poverty, dread, persecution with no place to call home. Now they rule with Christ in his exalted kingdom. The truth might be observed that the eternal society is quite different in its expectation and values than the kingdom of this world. We might all pray the words of Jesus, "Thy kingdom come"—a kingdom in which the first shall be last. In Revelation those in last position are celebrated for a thousand years.

At the end of the thousand years, Satan is released and tries one more time to overthrow the Lamb and his forces. John takes the term Gog of Magog and turns it into two nations Gog and Magog. Like Ezekiel, one finds that the final battle of Gog follows the messianic reign and predates the emergence of a new Jerusalem. From Ezek 38:6, we learn that Magog is a territory located to the far north of Israel. It should be viewed as theological geography—the place of the enemy of God's people. Hence, the battle symbolizes the victory of Christ over the ancient enemies of the saints of God.

The battle of Gog and Magog never really begins, for fire comes down from heaven and consumes the armies, and Satan is placed into the lake of fire with the beast and the false prophet. As we have said earlier, there is no real duality in Revelation. Satan's end is the lake of fire. Who can resist the power of the Lamb? Satan has tried all his power plays and assembled all his armies and absolutely no ground is gained. In God's world there is no place for evil. John symbolizes this struggle between good and evil as an actual battle between Satan and Christ. Yet the reader, by this time is well aware that it cannot be a battle of any consequence—Satan is doomed to failure even as evil cannot possibly persevere. Throughout Revelation proleptic scenes have shown us the triumph of God over the unrighteous. Thus no one can be very surprised by Satan's overwhelming defeat at the battle of Gog and Magog.

A sermon on the Gog and Magog passage, I would call "Jerusalem Besieged." The righteous way is always under attack. Jerusalem, the holy city is always under siege. At the very moment when all appears safe for the saints (the millennium) then a fresh attack is made upon the city. One might point out that the Christian life style like Jerusalem is always under siege. Have the meek ever inherited anything? What blessing comes from being merciful? Can one really love his/her neighbor? The siege often comes in terms of showing the impossibility of the Christian life style. Can the holy Jerusalem really stand in the midst of a desolate land? The believer can never presume that the last struggle has been fought. The Christian way is a day by day struggle to set forth the justice and love of God in the land. Hatred, injustice, and war are always nearby waiting to obliterate the holy city in moral darkness.

Hell or Gehenna is never mentioned in Revelation. Instead, one encounters a new word for the eternal place of punishment—the lake of fire. In any case, the lake of fire seems to be described in a similar way as Gehenna elsewhere in the NT. Sometimes it is described as a place of fire; other times as a place of "weeping and gnashing of teeth." In Revelation it is most of all a place called the second death (2:11; 20:6; 20:14; 21:8). The martyrs and the righteous receive eternal life but the followers of Satan receive an eternal death of torment and pain. For John only the righteous receive the gift of eternal life. In the OT creation story a human being is a living *nephesh* because the breath of God is breathed into him. When the human dies he becomes a dead *nephesh* for the breath of God is removed from him. Thus ultimately the lake of fire is eternal punishment—absence from God or spiritual death. No pain or torment could be worse than that.

Fulfillment of Judgment (20:11-15)

Following the final defeat of Satan, a general resurrection takes place and the "dead, great and small" stand before God's throne (the rest of the dead from 20:5). Every human being receives a just review of his life from the Divine Judge. The righteous are designated to rule in the new Jerusalem along with the martyrs. The expectation existed among the Jews that God kept books in which were recorded the good and bad deeds of human beings. Daniel declared, "The court sat in judgment and the books were opened" (7:10). The Israelites may have picked up the idea of a Book of Life from their Babylonian captivity. There a book containing the names of tax paying citizens bore that name. Other apocalyptic works mention record books which God keeps concerning the deeds of men (Enoch 90:20, IV Ezra 6:20; Apocalypse of Baruch 24:1). It is evident that John has in mind several books—record books of deeds and "a Book of Life" containing the names of the redeemed. The judgment which God ultimately makes concerning those before him is whether they are followers of the Lamb and have their names in the Book of Life.

These final scenes in Revelation lend themselves to a sermon on "The Book of the Living." (1) True life comes from an indepth relationship with the Lamb. Life is a gift from God which is breathed into man. (2) Immortality is also a gift that must be granted to us. Man's destiny is death and the grave. The book that God consults is the "book of the living ones"—those who have found quality life now and have the assurance of that for the future. (3) Perhaps John could have also included a "book of the dead"—containing the names of those who have followed the way of hatred and destruction. They have no hope before them, for they are doomed to the second death. In the Book of Life, the very best qualities of human life are found. In the book of death one finds the very worst.

Following the judgment scene, death and Hades, as the realm of death are destroyed. In our world which is so besieged by death, it is even difficult to think of a time when death will be destroyed. We often hear people talk of the power of death, but Revelation shows that death itself will have an end and its sway over mankind will be concluded. John views death and Hades in a personified fashion. In Revelation 6:7-8, death was represented by the pale green horse and Hades followed behind swallowing up the dead. Preaching values in this passage center in the theme of the limited power of death. Death itself is an evil force which must perish with the forces of Satan. One might point out that it is very fitting that death should be thrown into the lake of fire which is called the "second death."

Fulfillment of Heaven and Earth (21:1-3)

The Third Vision is directed to the redeemed and the righteous from the face of the earth. The promise manifests a new heaven and a new earth. As John portrayed the last judgment, he said, "From his presence earth and sky fled away, and no place was found for them" (20:11). Earth itself has fallen prey to man's sin and thus participates in his judgment. In John's view the old earth would be transformed and purged of its evil. The earth is redeemed even as man has been redeemed. Many other apocalypses paint a similar scene (I Enoch 45:4-5; 72:1; 91:16; II Esdras 7:75).

The beauty and peace of God's throne room as described in chapter five, now pervade the whole universe. The persecution and pain which the Christians experienced have passed away. A new age of great joy has dawned for believers. It is like the rays of the sun bursting forth out of a dark thundercloud. The great harlot has perished, the beast has been destroyed, and Satan has been cast into the lake of fire. The great eternity of peace has begun its reign. There will be no more earthquakes, tornadoes, floods, hurricanes, hail storms or drought. God's creation is now good as he intended for it to be from the beginning.

The suffering and pain in the world has caused human beings to ask many questions of God. From Job to C.S. Lewis, human beings have wondered if God is really concerned with the plight of man. For many persons the thought that God "really does not care" is perhaps a worse conclusion than that God does not really exist. However, John presents God as changing a fallen decayed order into a healed one in which once again he can demonstrate his love of mankind. The preacher might do a sermon on this passage called, "Does God Care?" and stress the following points: (1) We do not know all the answers of why human beings suffer. (2) We cannot possibly begin to provide the answers like Job's three friends were so eager to do. (3) Yet we do have the promise that the fallen order in which somehow the whole world participates will be transformed on the last day.

The new Jerusalem, the holy city descends from heaven and symbolizes the presence of God in his new creation. Much as in Genesis, God will once again walk in the midst of his people. The new Jerusalem seems to represent the last of the temple themes in Revelation. From the measurements given (21:15–17) we know that it is cubical in shape, just like the Holy of Holies in the heavenly temple. Thus, the temple themes which have appeared in each of the seven sections of Revelation reach their climax. In fact we are told by John that there is no need for a temple in the new Jerusalem—God will be in the midst of his people. The Holy of Holies descending to earth then carries with it the message that the elaborate temple structure is no longer needed. "Behold, the dwelling of God is with men. He will dwell with them, and they shall be his people, and God himself will be with them" (21:3).

In a message entitled "The Fellowship of the Redeemed," the proclaimer might point out several ideas based on this passage: (1) The fellowship will be with kindred spirits. In some way all will have been tested and tried through persecution and trials on earth. (2) All will have confessed allegiance to the Lamb and made his way the center of their lives. (3) The fellowship will have its roots in eternal worship of God which will bring the deepest joy known to human beings. He will abide with his people, and they will know his presence as they have never known it before. The difficulties of the old age will fade away from their memories. God will be the source of all that is good and holy.

Fulfillment of Believers (21:4–8)

The Fourth Vision is in the form of a series of assurances given to the believers who will inherit the new world.

(1) The first assurance is that the old enemy of man, pain, will be no more. One of the most tormenting plagues of man is the physical pain that comes with disease. Many have experienced the anguish of watching a relative or friend suffer with a terminal illness knowing that there is really nothing to be done to relieve the agony of their pain. The early Christian martyrs experienced the horrible pain that comes with being burned alive or thrown to wild animals. In addition to physical suffering, there is also the inner anguish of the spirit sometimes referred to as a "broken heart." Mental anguish can be as painful as physical pain. Probably the most poignant form of this kind of anguish is expressed in terms of mourning the death of a close friend. All societies have created rather elaborate rituals for dealing with this kind of sorrow or grief. In ancient Palestine mourning lasted for weeks and was especially given to women to carry out since they were held responsible for bringing sin into the world. Jewish women were even hired to cry at funerals and to accompany the corpse to the tomb.

In the new Jerusalem, the promise is given that there will be no more pain and weeping. It is difficult for modern people to even conceive of such a paradise. Without some view of life after death or resurrection, the cruelty of the world would not make sense. The view of God in this passage does not represent some startling new revelation—it has been with us all along. God has sought throughout history to wipe away the tears from the eyes of mankind. The freedom which God gives to us also allows us to turn from him and go our own ways. The decay and fallen state of the world, the biblical narrative attributes to man. In his love, God is seeking to redeem the universe and create a world in which there is no more pain and suffering. Death itself has been conquered.

(2) The biblical world was one which knew well the specter of thirst. Water has always been in short supply in Palestine. So many of the Old Testament narratives revolve around wells, for a supply of water is well worth fighting over. When

Jesus pondered an analogy to express the longing for the kingdom of God, he spoke of "to hunger and thirst" for it. Throughout Revelation emphasis has been placed quite often on rivers and springs of water. In fact one of the last images in the Apocalypse is of a river of life flowing from the throne of God. John presents God as the Alpha and the Omega, the beginning and end. Thus he is able to be the source of living water that will end all thirst. Jesus once reminded the woman at the well of a water that provided the end of the need to drink—a water that conquered thirst. A sermon called "No More Thirst" might contrast man's constant search for water to the abundant water available in God's city.

(3) Once again John assures the saints that all evil will be absent from the city. "But as for the cowardly, the faithless, the polluted, as for murderers, fornicators, sorcerers, idolaters, and all liars, their lot shall be in the lake that burns with fire and sulphur, which is the second death" (21:8). It is as if John himself can hardly believe this assurance. He adds it almost as a footnote to the other more positive assurances. It is like waking from a beautiful dream and wondering if what you experienced is still real. A world without the various evils mentioned in verse eight is difficult to comprehend. Almost all these ills enumerated here are related to following the beasts. At the top of the list is the word "cowardly." Those who celebrate with God in heaven are those who were not afraid to stand up to the beast and resist its evil influence. A sermon "Moral Cowards" might deal with the reluctance of some Christians to confront evil in our world. One might use the illustration of the proliferation of atomic weapons on our planet. Many Christian groups have begun to realize that speaking out against the abuse of atomic weapons is a genuine Christian concern. Yet others find it easier to accept the "arms race" as a necessity to preserve the status quo. It takes courage to stand up for a concern and fight hard to see it persevere. The coward is always despised in every human society. They are the ones who shrink back from any kind of risk and are always seeking safe ground and calm waters. The eternal kingdom of God is made up of those who are willing to die for the kingdom. "He who conquers shall have this heritage" (21:7).

Fulfillment of the New Jerusalem (21:9-21)

The new Jerusalem itself becomes the center of attention in the Fifth Vision. In chapter four, John described the appearance of God as a jasper jewel. Now, as John is shown the new Jerusalem descending from the heavens, the jasper is used once again to describe God—"having the glory of God, its radiance like a most rare jewel, like a jasper, clear as crystal" (21:11). As we have said earlier, the new Jerusalem is the Holy of Holies, God's dwelling place. He will "tabernacle" with us. The description of the city is intended to heighten the impression of God's presence among his people. So often Christians take the depiction of the holy city here and present heaven as a very materialistic place. Some interpreters will insist on seeing images and symbols elsewhere in Revelation but suddenly become very literal in interpretation at the point of the new Jerusalem.

The preacher should make an attempt to find the meaning and message in the rich symbols of this section. In verse twelve, we are told that the city has twelve gates with the names of the twelve tribes upon them. Twelve foundation stones underlie the walls of the city. The names of the twelve disciples are inscribed upon them. In these symbols, we find the message that the holy city is built upon the promises of God—his covenants established with his people. The twelve tribes represent the old covenant and the twelve disciples the new covenant. In chapter four, the same symbolism is apparent in the twenty-four elders around the throne of God—the twelve disciples and the twelve tribes of Israel. Thus we find the truth that the very city rests upon the covenants of God.

Next of all John is told to measure the city. It is interesting to note the number of modern English translations that attempt to update John's measurements into present day miles and feet. In doing so, the symbolism of the numbers is lost. For example, the city is said to be 12,000 stadia by 12,000 by 12,000—roughly a cube. The number twelve represents wholeness. The basic truth is the same as expressed in the Gospel of John, "In my Father's house are many rooms" (14:2). The literal measurement of the city is not as important as the spiritual truth. God's city is large enough for all true believers. The size of the walls is sufficient to secure it as well. The number used in the wall measurements is based on 144, a multiple of twelve. The walls symbolize the security of God's presence for the believers.

Precious jewels are used throughout the description to emphasize the striking beauty of the city. It is like beholding a beautiful rose on a spring morning and attempting to describe it in writing. All human words fail in trying to recapture the beauty of the rose. At best one needs poetry to express the beauty in words of the rose. In addition twelve precious stones serve as a foundation for the city. They may correspond to the twelve precious stones on the breastplate of the high priest. R. H. Charles (*Revelation*) has argued that these stones were used in the ancient world for the twelve signs of the Zodiac, and that John reversed their order to negate the impact of astrological worship.

1. Jasper—Pisces
2. Sapphire—Aquarius
3. Agate—Capricorn
4. Emerald—Sagittarius
5. Onyx—Scorpion
6. Carnelian—Libra
7. Chrysolite—Virgo
8. Beryl—Leo
9. Topaz—Cancer
10. Chrysoprase—Gemini
11. Jacinth—Taurus
12. Amethyst—Aries

John wants the world to know that the true celestial city has its foundations in God and in the Lamb. The names of the twelve disciples on the foundation stones symbolize their testimony to God's revelation in Christ.

In a sermon called "Foundations of Faith," one should attempt to capture the symbolic messages of John's description of the new Jerusalem. The first point could deal with the measurement of the city—it is large enough for all. Our Christian faith rests on the promise that God's love is for all people. The message of Christ has always been universalistic in nature. The second point might develop the concept of the security which a life of faith assures. The city's wall is based on the number twelve—wholeness. The final point might deal with the foundation stones. Our faith rests upon the testimony of the disciples and provides the true way to God.

Fulfillment of Divine Light (21:22–27)

The Sixth Vision promises divine illumination of the city. "And the city has no need of sun or moon to shine upon it, for the glory of God is its light, and its lamp is the Lamb" (21:23). Darkness today is not as feared as it was in the ancient world. Today, many people are unaware of the change from day to night. The artificially controlled climates of our modern buildings call for structures without windows. Thus darkness and light are not so important anymore. However, in the ancient world darkness was usually portrayed as a monster—something to be greatly feared and avoided. A source of light in most homes was expensive. The olive oil used in a lamp could be better put to cooking purposes or other functions. A first-century Palestinian city would not be aglow with light like one of our modern cities.

Thus, a city aglow with the light of the Lamb would boggle the imagination of a first century reader of Revelation. Something of that feeling comes upon the modern reader when he flies at night over a great city like London or New York. It appears as if the whole world is ablaze with light. "The Light which Penetrates Darkness" might be a good title for a sermon here. The first point could deal with the Christological title, light of the world. In many senses, the world lay in darkness until the incarnation of light in Jesus Christ. The second point might emphasize the cross as an eternal source of light for the whole world. There darkness perceived the power of light and capitulated. The third point should stress the final victory of light over darkness in the new Jerusalem. Darkness is destroyed forever.

John also relates to us that the gates of the city are always open. The nations that once opposed the Lamb will now enter the gates to bow down and worship him. The whole created order including the structure of nations has been redeemed. There is no force outside the power of God. John's view rests heavily on Isaiah 60:11:

> Your gates shall be open continually;
>   day and night they shall not be shut;
> that men may bring to you the wealth of the nations
>   with their kings led in procession.

Fulfillment of Divine Life (22:1–5)

The river of life is the focus of attention in the Seventh Vision. John relies directly here on the Garden of Eden narrative in Genesis. In the Garden, a river goes forth from Eden

(Gen 2:10) and in Revelation, a river emerges from the throne of God. As in Eden, there is a tree or trees of life in the new Jerusalem. From the description there seems to be trees on both sides of the river. We find a similar picture in Ezekiel.

> And on the banks, on both sides of the river, there will grow all kinds of trees for food. Their leaves will not wither nor their fruit fail, but they will bear fresh fruit every month, because the water for them flows from the sanctuary. Their fruit will be for food, and their leaves for healing" (47:12).

John seems to have taken the one tree of life from Genesis and developed an avenue of such trees on each side of the river like the fruit trees in Ezekiel. In a similar vein also, the leaves of these trees of life are used for the healing of the nations. The symbols of trees of life and water of life show the great emphasis which John places upon the abundant life available for believers in the new Jerusalem.

In a sermon entitled "The Great Physician," one might develop the theme of healing in this passage. (1) There is the healing which frees the redeemed from the scars of their former life marked by persecution and pain. The struggle with evil leaves its inevitable scars. (2) There is also the healing which comes from physical disease. Those believers who have been ravaged by disease find wholeness in the healing balm available in the Lamb. (3) Another healing may be seen in the wholeness which comes to human living. The tree of life affords to those who eat of its fruit a total picture of what life is all about. Life without the Lamb is broken into hundreds of pieces. The great physician works his cure through the symbol of the Tree of Life. He is Lord over life and manifests life in its fullness.

At the center of the city stands the throne of God. In a very dramatic point in his story the man of Patmos declares, "they shall see his face" (22:4). Even Moses did not dare to look upon the face of God. Now in the total unity of man with God, the face of God will not be something to fear but rather the central force and power of the new age. The face of God, of course, is most clearly viewed in the Lamb, Jesus Christ. "The Many Faces of God" is a title of a sermon dealing with the way God has tried to approach men throughout history. (1) in the OT, it is a Hebrew face as God sought to reveal himself in one nation who in turn would be a light to the world. (2) In the NT, God's face is the face of Jesus Christ manifesting his love and mercy to mankind. (3) In the new Jerusalem his face is reflected in the glory and beauty of eternal fellowship with his people.

Epilogue
(Revelation 22:6–21)

The closing words of Revelation serve as a summary of the basic ideas presented throughout the book. John is concerned especially with the practical application of the underlying message of his Apocalypse. This section is loosely written and held together by the barest outline. One of the most difficult things is to determine the identity of the various speakers in this last chapter of Revelation. It almost seems as if John is bringing back all his major characters for one final statement before the curtain falls on his drama.

The Authenticity of the Prophet

The angels throughout Revelation have interpreted God's message to John. The purpose of this final angelic announcement is to give added credence to John's testimony and writing. God is described as "the God of the spirits of the prophets" (22:6). Right away, John's words have been linked to the testimonies of the great Hebrew prophets like Jeremiah and Ezekiel. Indeed the sixth "blessing" of the Apocalypse intentionally refers to John's words as prophecy: "Blessed is he who keeps the words of the prophecy of this book" (22:7). Thus whoever hears the words of Revelation must give heed to them as divine and worthy of obedience.

John's role as prophet is further underlined in 22:8–9 where the seer falls down before the angel to offer him worship. The angel rejects such manifestations and identifies himself as "a fellow servant with you and your brethren the prophets" (v.9). This type of statement would be very important at the conclusion of a book which would be read aloud in churches. By the end of the first century A.D. many writings were in circulation in the Christian communities of Asia Minor. Some of these works included heretical ideas or doctrines that would endanger the fellowship. In contrast, John's visions were given of God through a heavenly messenger and bore the imprint of the divine Word itself.

The pastor might consider here a sermon based on three of

the "blessings" in Revelation which deal with taking heed to God's Word. We could call this sermon "The Blessings of God's Word": (a) blessed is he who reads aloud (1:3), (b) blessed is he who keeps the words (22:7), and (c) blessed is he who is awake (16:15). In point (a) one might point out that all three blessings are outlined in 1:3, but restated in 22:7 and 16:15. The words of John would first be read aloud in the congregations of Asia Minor. Obedience of God's word first begins with its hearing. John has done much in Revelation to use dramatic patterns that will enable those who hear Revelation read aloud to experience something of what he saw and heard. Of course point (b) would lead one into the realm of obedience of the Word. These are not just words of any writer, they are prophetic words spoken by God to John. The third point (c) calls for the readers to be watchful and underline John's basic concern with the return of Christ, God's Word ultimately will be confirmed by the return of Christ in glory.

The Imminence of the End

Another major voice in the Epilogue is the voice of Jesus Christ which rings out with fervent eschatological hope in these concluding verses of Revelation: "Behold, I am coming soon" (22:7–12). We are told again in 22:10 that "the time is near." In fact the end is so close that there is no time remaining to change radically the life patterns of human beings: "Let the evildoer still do evil" (22:11). It is now time for those who have opposed God to reap the harvest of their unconcern. The announcement of the soon return of Christ is answered by the anguished cry of the Christian believers of Asia Minor, "Amen, Come, Lord Jesus!" (22:20).

These concluding words of Christ might give rise to a sermon on eschatological hope. The title might well be, "Come, Lord Jesus": (a) behold, I am coming soon (22:12), (b) bringing my recompense (22:12b), and (c) blessed are those who wash their robes (22:14). The first point (a) might emphasize the hope of the Christian church that Christ is both the Alpha and Omega. Just as the beginning of history is founded upon God's initiative so also will be its conclusion. In the second point of the sermon (b) the theme of judgment should be stressed. The return of Christ brings a division between those who have been true followers and those who have followed the way of evil. The righteous will receive entrance into the heavenly city and access to the tree of life (22:14). Those who have devoted themselves to evil, "dogs and sorcerers and fornicators and murderers and idolators" (22:15) are outside the city. For John eschatological hope brings with it decision and separation. The third point (c) emphasizes the need to stay in preparation for the imminent return of Christ. A blessing is bestowed upon those who "wash their robes" (22:14). Whenever the Word of God is preached and proclaimed, the hearer must respond in an eschatological manner—either to accept the proclaimed Christ or to reject him. If the hearer acknowledges the living Christ, his life style reflects Christ's message of love. "Let him who desires take the water of life without price" (22:17).

The Words of Warning

John, the third figure also has some concluding words in Revelation. In 22:8, he identifies himself with the central figure of his book: "I John am he who heard and saw these things" (22:8). In addition he adds a very stiff warning to his work:

> I warn every one who hears the words of the prophecy of this book: if any one adds to them, God will add to him the plagues described in this book, and if any one takes away from the words of the prophecy, God will take away his share in the tree of life and in the holy city, which are described in this book (22:18-19).

Apocalyptic literature relies so heavily upon numbers, colors, and animals that any slight change in these patterns would alter its basic message. Enoch declares that no one should "change or diminish ought of my words" (104:10). It is also a claim to be the word of God and equal with the Hebrew scriptures. These words however were not directed primarily to some future generation but to those Christians in the seven churches who would hear Revelation read aloud in their communities and must accept its basic teaching as the Gospel.

These themes contained in the final warning of Revelation might be treated in a sermon entitled "The Gospel: Adding and Subtracting." In the first point, one might deal with the attempts throughout history to add to the basic Gospel. The Judaizers of Galatia, for example, desired to add the rigid requirements of the law to the Gospel's message of grace. Secondly, we also encounter historical attempts to subtract from the impact of the Gospel. Somehow, God's grace is never sufficient to include all persons or all races or both sexes or really all sinners. Thirdly, one might emphasize that there is only *one* Gospel. Paul once declared, "For I would have you know, brethren, that the gospel which was preached by me is not man's gospel" (Gal 1:11). The divine Gospel can never be changed into a human gospel, for in that case that which is eternal and universal would become mortal and limited.

Bibliography

For those interested in the dramatic approach to Revelation, further reading suggestions would include John Wick Bowman, *The First Christian Drama* (Philidelphia: Westminster Press, 1965) and James L. Blevins, "The Genre of Revelation," *Review and Expositor* (Vol. LXXVIII, Summer, 1980). The best commentaries include the classic work of Ibson T. Beckwith, *The Apocalypse of John* (Grand Rapids: Baker Book House, 1919, 1979). The best recent works certainly would be found in G. R. Caird, *The Revelation of St. John Divine* (New York: Harper & Row, 1966); G. R. Beasley-Murray *The Book of Revelation* (Greenwood, SC: Attic Press, Inc., 1974). Two popular commentaries which would be helpful to recommend to lay persons would be Elisabeth Fiorenza, *Invitation to the Book of Revelation* (Garden City, NY: Image Books, 1981), and Richard L. Jeske, *Revelation for Today* (Philadelphia: Fortress Press, 1983). The best help on the seven churches comes from the old classic, William Ramsey, *The Letters to the Seven Churches* (Grand Rapids: Baker Book House, 1908, 1979) and the newer work: Otto Meinardus, *St. John of Patmos and the Seven Churches of the Apocalypse* (Athens: Lycabettus Press, 1974).

Note: he never mentions E. A. McDowell's The Meaning and Message of the Book of Revelation (Broadman, 1951)